I0823027

BUDGET LUXURY

BSG

BUDGET LUXURY

YOUR GUIDE TO CREATING A BEAUTIFUL HOME WITHOUT BREAKING THE BANK

CLARE SULLIVAN

PHOTOGRAPHS BY
NIKKI HIRST

ILLUSTRATIONS BY
CLARE SULLIVAN

RODALE
NEW YORK

Rodale Books
An imprint of Random House
A division of Penguin Random House LLC
1745 Broadway, New York, NY 10019
rodalebooks.com | randomhousebooks.com
penguinrandomhouse.com

Library of Congress Cataloging-in-Publication Data
Names: Sullivan, Clare, MFA author
Title: Budget luxury / Clare Sullivan; photographs by Nikki Hirst.
Description: New York, NY: Rodale, [2026]
Identifiers: LCCN 2025024682 (print) | LCCN 2025024683 (ebook) |
ISBN 9780593798102 hardcover | ISBN 9780593798119 ebook
Subjects: LCSH: Interior decoration
Classification: LCC NK2110 .S93 2026 (print) |
LCC NK2110 (ebook) | DDC 747—dc23/eng/20250807
LC record available at https://lccn.loc.gov/2025024682
LC ebook record available at https://lccn.loc.gov/2025024683

Printed in China

9 8 7 6 5 4 3 2 1

First Edition

BOOK TEAM:
Editor: Dervla Kelly
Editorial Assistant: Emi Harris
Art Director: Jenny Davis
Designer: Lynne Yeamans
Managing Editor: Allie Fox
Production Editor: Robert Siek
Production Manager: Jennifer Backe
Copy Editor: Robin Slutzky
Proofreaders: Amy Harned, Muriel Jorgensen, Karina Jha, and Tess Rossi

Cover art by Shutterstock: Olga Kovalenko (paperclip), My Life Graphic (paper beneath color swatches), Lifestyle Graphic (ripped journal paper), Bankrx (color swatches), Wachiwit (blue tape at top), Sirina F (blue tape at bottom)

Cover and endpaper pattern illustrations by Clare Sullivan

Endpaper art by Shutterstock: Wachiwit (blue tape), onair (torn paper)

The authorized representative in the EU for product safety and compliance is Penguin Random House Ireland, Morrison Chambers, 32 Nassau Street, Dublin D02 YH68. Ireland. https://eu-contact.penguin.ie

To my son, Myles: Your arrival turned my entire world Technicolor.

And to my husband, Brian, my best friend. I love you.

CONTENTS

INTRODUCTION

A few years ago, I could not have predicted that I'd be an interior design content creator. My job didn't even exist when I was in school. But it turns out, my weird job is the perfect one for me. Let me tell you, I didn't ever think I would find my "dream job." In my mid-twenties, I was living in New York, aimlessly working in a job that made me totally miserable, but didn't know how to get "unstuck."

A particular memory from those days remains with me today. I was crying and exhausted one evening in my Alphabet City apartment, having reached that critical rock-bottom at which I could either swim back up to the surface or drown in my current reality. I was working at my second job after graduating college—a low-level associate gig for a public relations firm specializing in the most niche thing ever: financial advisers. PR was easy enough to get a grasp of, but finance?! Not only was I completely confused by the industry I was supposed to understand, but I was also incredibly bored by it. I was feeling like my life was a lost cause.

Back to that hot night on Avenue C: I can still feel the too-dry wood of the IKEA kitchen table under my hands, which dripped with sweat from damp city heat . . . My lampshade, off-kilter, glowed Halloween-orange from the lightbulb I'd bought months earlier as a party prop. I can still hear the wailing of sirens unsubdued by the flimsy partition wall my roommate and I had put up to create two tiny sleeping areas in a one-bedroom apartment.

That partition wall was actually one of my first design projects. My roommate, Paige, was also my best friend from childhood. Even though we were like sisters and never shied away from sharing a bed, I'd just spent the previous six months sharing a bedroom with another roommate on Saint Marks Place, where my college friends and I had piled in after graduation to save money. Needless to say, I was ready for my own space, and we were thrilled to be living in our first "big girl" apartment. So we did what any recent college grad living in New York City does: called up the "wall guy." I sketched a floor plan of our living room area and showed him where to put the temporary

OPPOSITE: On a site visit with my son, Myles.

wall that would create my new bedroom. I even remember skipping down to the hardware store to pick out a robin's-egg blue to paint it. Memories of creative joy, like these, contrast with the many nights I spent coming home from work crying.

Back to that one particular night: At this point, I was so fed up with crying over my life that I decided to make an immediate change. I grabbed a pen and a piece of scrap paper. Though I'd never allowed myself to fully embrace my creativity, that night something magical happened: My hands took over as if enchanted. I began to sketch, not knowing what the tear-blotched pen lines I was scribbling across the paper would become. After about five minutes of frantic drawing, I studied the sketch I'd drawn. I felt, for the first time in ages, hopeful.

This is a re-creation of my scrap paper sketch from that dark night, that I WISH I'd saved. Thankfully, it's still a clear image in my mind, and a future I'm still in the process of striving for.

I had drawn a two-story shack, covered in shingles and elevated on whimsical stilts. The double doors to the shack were arched and flung open. Above them hung a crooked sign with my very own name on it. On the first floor, there were products lining the walls, and a gigantic flower bouquet perched on a round table in the middle of what appeared to be a home decor store. Upstairs, stick figure Clare was working at a drafting desk surrounded by rolls of floor plans and a computer displaying her very own website.

I didn't really know what I was looking at, but I knew I wanted to be there, living in that scene I'd drawn. I asked myself, for the first time in my life, "What do I want to do?" I'd been asked this question loads of times by my parents, my teachers, and my friends. But I'd never asked it of myself. This time, I asked without pressuring myself that my answer had to be a fancy job title or "Save the world." I just wanted to answer it correctly.

Underneath my little sketch, I wrote:

"I just want to make everything around me beautiful."

And I knew instantly that I needed to do just that. That mantra has become a personal compass that gives me direction in life. Apart from my family, it's my most important cornerstone; the phrase I can lean on if ever I feel lost or unsure of the future.

The very next day, I applied to interior design graduate programs in the city. My parents didn't understand why I'd throw my steady, paying job out the window for something so risky and uncertain. Miraculously, I got into all three of the New York design programs I'd applied to. I remember opening my acceptance letter to Parsons in the lobby of my building, too nervous to wait until I got inside my apartment. I read the letter in complete shock: Not only was I accepted, but they had offered me their president's scholarship, which covered 75 percent of my tuition. Turns out, my undergrad art portfolio wasn't a complete waste of time!

To cover the remaining 25 percent of tuition costs, I landed a job at a high-end cabinetry shop, which exposed me to the world of luxury interior design. I walked from Parsons to my job on 10th Street each day, where I got to work with celebrities, famous interior designers, and even billionaire video game creators. (By "work with," I mean . . . I got them coffee.) Most of my fellow students didn't work, since our curriculum was so intense, but I didn't have the choice. Though it was grueling, learning how to balance a job and school taught me how to work hard for something I wanted.

At the cabinetry shop, our clients' multimillion-dollar interior design budgets blew my mind—and that was just the tip of the iceberg. I was captivated by the beauty and grandeur of it all, and I became a sponge on the job, soaking up as much information as I could. I fell in love with luxe paint colors, learned to pronounce the French names of fancy wallpaper houses, and studied the opulent rooms of top interior designers.

At home after late-night studio sessions at Parsons, I'd open a copy of *Architectural Digest* or watch lavish home tours on YouTube. I was enamored with the beautiful homes that money could create, but I couldn't shake a feeling of unease.

A dreamy sketch from my early twenties.

I'd look around at my own slapped-together apartment, filled with hand-me-down furniture and framed art I'd printed at Staples. I yearned for a more beautiful space. "Why does luxury interior design have to be so inaccessible?" I kept asking.

It's a question I explored throughout my two years at Parsons. One of my favorite projects proposed an aesthetically beautiful mobile farmers market to help food-desert areas in Brooklyn by using low-cost, sustainable materials. My professors pushed me to investigate how

"IT TOOK ME SOME TIME TO FIND MYSELF, AND ONCE I DID, MY STYLE FOLLOWED."

good design could be accessible to all. They encouraged me to dismantle the reasons why good design, which is such a crucial part of our well-being, is off-limits to the average person and blocked from public consumption with red-velvet-rope barriers.

In the years that followed my graduation from Parsons, I decided to work for myself.

Creative entrepreneurship wasn't really something I chose; it was something I simply couldn't ignore. It was an itch I knew I needed to scratch. My creative fuel gets supercharged by one thing: problem solving.

An obstacle presents a problem, and a problem demands a solution. And I always want to reach that solution. It may sound counter-intuitive, but my creativity runs on lack: lack of materials, lack of space, lack of budget.

My philosophy of creativity is the same one I apply to budgeting. I think of a low budget not as an interior design obstacle, but as a problem that needs solving. I can confidently say that I create better designs on a limited budget than if I had a million dollars to spend. Because not only do limited budgets create more interesting solutions, but they also invite a much more personal approach to design. A good interior is full of love, effort, and personal effects. Good design is that which reflects YOU: your heart, your travels, your passions. I've found that you don't need a big budget to achieve good design—what you need is the confidence to design your home as an extension of your truest self.

It took me some time to find myself, and once I did, my style followed. I promise we can get you there, too.

I learned a lot about myself and design in the past few years, and in this book I'm going to teach you that:

- Beautiful interior design doesn't have to be inaccessible.
- A lovely home is created by self-expression, not by throwing wads of money at an expensive interior designer.
- If you can tell me who you are in words, you can tell me who you are through your design style.

If you're willing to dust off your tools, get thrifty, and dive deep to explore your own personal story, then you're well on your way to creating the #BudgetLuxury home of your dreams. And I'm so excited for us to roll up our sleeves and get creative together!

I'm happiest at home, where I am surrounded by my favorite patterns, curios, and artwork.

USING THIS BOOK

If you bought this book, I'm guessing you're not a professional interior designer. But here's a secret—neither am I! Yes, I have an education in the subject, but my unorthodox career path isn't guided by the goal of signing high-paying clients or publishing my designs in magazines. Instead, it's guided by my desire to help people create beauty with their own two hands. Each day, I wake up with creative ideas swirling in my head, and I have an innate and unshakable desire to share those ideas in the hope that they'll inspire others to try something new. I'd call myself more of an *idea* designer than an *interior* designer.

That said, this book isn't a photo album of dazzling rooms I've designed. I won't be telling you what fabric to buy for your drapes or giving you a lecture about which throw pillows look best against a blue couch. Though you could save those questions for a real interior designer, my goal is to empower you to make these personal design decisions for yourself. I mean, every time I hear an anecdote from a friend or family member about hiring an interior designer, it usually doesn't have a great outcome. I hear more stories about fired interior designers than I do about hired interior designers. I believe this is because, deep down, *you* know what you like. You do have an eye. And your style is special, because it's different from anyone else's. Your unique life experiences have led you to developing your very own interior designer eye. Which is why you're able to watch HGTV and totally judge the reveal at the end of the episode. And although right now you may not have the experience to execute a beautifully layered living room, once you learn a few important things about yourself, you'll be much more confident in your design abilities.

With this book, I'm giving you all the resources and tools you'll need to become your very own interior designer. As a creative person, people come to me for advice about their home, claiming they have no idea what they're doing "when it comes to this stuff." Instead of *telling* them which furniture catalogs to shop or where they should put their dining table, I *ask* them questions about what they like and dislike. For example, when my mother-in-law asked me for guidance concerning a section of her family room, I didn't hand her a design scheme and a shopping list—instead, I asked about her *intentions* with the problem area in question:

OPPOSITE: Are you ready to transform your space on a budget?!

MY MOTHER-IN-LAW'S FAMILY ROOM

How do you feel about the area in terms of use—what purpose does it serve?
Well, it's in front of the sliding doors. So, it's more of a walkway than anything else. Right now it's just dead space, and nobody actually works at the desk since it's so small and in the middle of everyone's path coming in and out of the backyard.

What do you like about the space?
I like the symmetry of the two walls on either side of the sliding door.

What don't you like?
I want this house to feel light and airy. But the black shelves and desk that are there now feel so heavy. I don't like the utilitarian rug we have down right now. I know I want a rug there, but I want it to be cute. Maybe blue, to go with the rest of the decor in here.

Okay, so let's swap that with a blue rug. Easy!
Yes, and if we do a blue rug, we'd probably want to add some blue art. But I think we should have some storage here, too.

I let her ponder . . .

Maybe we get rid of the black desk. Nobody uses it. And if the desk is gone, we have plenty of room for some storage.

You mentioned you liked the symmetry of the area . . . Could we emphasize that?
Some shallow bookcases would work. And placing one on each side of the room would highlight the symmetry. We'd be able to display art on them *and* use them for storage. And I think we should go with white since I'm trying for that bright and airy look!

My mother-in-law possesses more taste than Queen Elizabeth, but she'd never admit that to others, let alone herself! Because she's not a certified interior designer, she wanted my help. But by answering a few simple questions, she was able to come up with a design scheme based on her own taste and needs. I didn't redesign my mother-in-law's room—she did! And I must say, it came out great.

"I have no idea what I'm doing" is just something hurtful you've told yourself for years! I think you'll find that after doing some soul-searching, you'll be able to make design decisions with confidence.

Maybe by now you're rolling your eyes. "Clare, not everyone has good taste!" you might be saying. And I get it. I've told myself for years that I'm bad at math . . . and I *am* bad at math. Truly and horrifyingly bad at math. 61 + 25? Couldn't tell ya. That's not going to change, and nothing is going to help me magically get better at multiplication. Oh, shit. That was addition. But anyway, taste is a different story.

Taste is inherent. We all walk through life with likes and dislikes. Maybe you don't like the taste of cilantro (weird of you, but whatever). You *know* you don't like cilantro. Your dislike of cilantro is an unwavering conviction that you feel confident in. You hate cilantro.

Now imagine you're at the grocrey store shopping for a Mexican meal. The recipe calls for cilantro. What are you going to do?

WELL, YOU'RE NOT BUYING THE CILANTRO.

Okay, I get it! You hate cilantro! Why are we still talking about it?! Oh, right, that's on me. The author. And now it's also on me to transition from cilantro to interior design proclivities. Hmm.

Let's take leopard print, which is similar to cilantro in its polarizing nature. You love it or you hate it. Don't give me that wishy-washy shrug! Nobody is indifferent about leopard print. Or cilantro.

Cilantro, love it or hate it!

NEXT TIME YOU FACE A DESIGN DILEMMA, ASK YOURSELF . . .

1. What do you like about the room, architecturally speaking, that you could emphasize?
2. What purpose does the room serve? Could it do a better job? If so, how?
3. What types of rooms do you save on Pinterest, or dog-ear in magazines? Are there color schemes and textures you feel naturally drawn to?
4. How do you want to feel when you're in this room? Could a muted palette help you relax? Would extra pillows make you feel more "at home"? Could the art you select transport you to another state of mind?
5. Pretend you're on a reality TV show. A crew of designers and contractors has twenty-four hours to renovate your "problem room." You fall asleep tonight and wake up to a totally transformed space. What does it look like?
6. What are you so afraid of?

TODAY
LET'S
PAINT™

Adorning my interior with personal objects is how I define myself.

If you hate it: fine. But please return this book and never talk to me again. You basically just said you hate me. Leopard is a neutral in my world.

I joke. You're forgiven—but guess what you just learned. You have TASTE! See, I made the connection between food and decor. It would have been easier to simply write about how everyone can taste their own food, thus everyone possesses their own design taste. But that'd be boring, and I want this book to be FUN!

If you're going to have fun with this book, you're going to have to embrace your inner creative genius. Maybe you're someone who knows they're creative—great! But if you, like so many people I know, tell yourself you're not creative *enough,* you have some unlearning to do. In my opinion, everyone can be creative. My own husband constantly says to me, "You're the creative one, I'm not creative . . . [blah blah husband voice blah]." And then, after all that, he has the nerve to style his bookcases in an unconventional and truly beautiful way! Seriously, you should see his office. He created a room that seems to have been decorated by an eighty-nine-year-old retired pirate. It's cool. I wouldn't tell him that in person, because I want him to stop buying antique whale teeth, but, Brian, if you're reading this—I'm proud of you.

Back to you, dear reader. Your homework is to unlearn the fear of judgment ingrained in your mind. Work on following your whims, even if that just means rearranging a shelf tonight. I want you to be brave. Embracing your own style requires bravery. But the good news is, it's much easier to be brave within the comfort of your own home than anywhere else! Be brave, embrace your taste, and get ready to create your dream home with your own two hands.

And when you start questioning whether you have any taste, ask yourself whether or not you like cilantro.

xo, Clare

MASTER CLASS IN WATERCOLOR
May I Come In?
WENDY GOODMAN
THE END MONTAUK, N.Y.
MICHAEL DWECK

TRENDS: THEY'RE NOT YOUR FRIENDS!

I hold tight to the belief that interior design should be personal. It should reflect who *you* are, at your core. Yet we've strayed so far from the concept of personal taste. I blame a few factors, and one of them is actually how I make my living—the internet! I don't love the title "influencer," as I try not to *influence* you to follow my design style. Instead, I hope to *inspire* you to try my ideas in your own personal style. And I'm not perfect in this regard. If I love something, I share it—and often with a commissionable link. While I willingly participate in the internet economy of our day and age, I can't help but have complicated feelings when it comes to influencing.

The internet's exhaustive, fast-paced churning of trends has created a pack-mentality generation of individuals who, in their quest for individualism, have lost any ounce of it. We turn to social media to tell us how to dress, what to eat, and how to decorate. Personal style, as it was, doesn't exist in our current zeitgeist. Instead, each micro-style that can be identified gets its own name: dark academia, cottagecore, quiet luxury, coastal grandma (my personal favorite, by the way!). Through our overclassification of style, uniqueness is eradicated. Recently, I was scrolling on my phone when I came across a home tour. The living room was impeccably original, as the homeowner had combined their own love of midcentury furniture with rococo art, pastel tones, and unexpected natural details. When I opened the comments, I wasn't at all surprised at what I saw. "User437289423: What are we calling this style??" "Designbrat42069: This is the bright decaying modern aesthetic." Because of social media, we stuff every "look" into a box these days. One of my favorite style descriptors, "whimsigothic," stands for "whimsical mystical Gothic celestial," referencing a late 1980s style mostly found in coffee shops and teenagers' bedrooms. The style encapsulates jewel tones, astrological iconography, stained-glass windows, and magical ephemera. Today, it's back in a big way as a design trend. Tomorrow, however, is a different story. Those who so enthusiastically bought faux-ivy vines and astrologically themed mobiles for their bedrooms will move on quickly to the next micro-trend, buying into the ideology that embracing a niche internet trend will also help them embrace their individuality. Unfortunately, due to an insecurity epidemic, we've turned to the internet to tell us *who* we are, *what* we like, and *how* we express ourselves.

OPPOSITE: To keep my home feeling fresh, I rejuvenate it seasonally using natural decor rather than constantly keeping up with trends.

Discovering your own "timeless style" can be as simple as leafing through old magazines rather than scrolling through your phone!

Who is more equipped to exploit this cultural phenomenon than big-box capitalism, with its armies of overseas factories, quick-ship innovations, and deep pockets? American retail has been quick to adapt to our fleeting-trend cycle. Fast fashion has been an issue for a few decades, but fast furniture is a more recent symptom of social media's clutch on the economy. Today, furniture companies embrace trendy labels in their advertisements: "Cottagecore bedding—on sale this week only!" It's a tempting offer, especially if you like dainty floral motifs. And though the corporatization of trends is nauseating, the original sources of these trends are often beautiful, unique, and tasteful.

When a favorite influencer of mine, Lex Nicoleta, coined the term "coastal grandmother," she referenced elegant yet understated traditional interiors, effortlessly beautiful Nancy Meyers movie sets, cozy sweaters, and even music—French jazz and sixties soul among the genres that encapsulate this aspirational lifestyle. I love the idea that a segment of zillennial and millennial women (myself included) identify with lifestyle customs previously reserved for elderly elite ladies living on Nantucket. It's comforting to feel camaraderie online, and style can be a great way to find community. Trends have always existed and have always been classified. Of course, we, while maintaining our individuality, are perfectly capable of gravitating toward certain styles. But after the "coastal grandmother" trend trickled through the sinuous membrane of the internet and into the mainstream, huge home decor retailers began using the term in their advertising efforts, pushing poorly made bedside tables and polyester throw pillows under its moniker. The commercial manipulation of our niche internet community's beloved aesthetic left me with a sour taste in my mouth.

So, dear reader, I encourage you to find your own way. Just because you like bright colors and tulips doesn't mean you need to define yourself under the "Copenhagen decor" aesthetic. You might also like early American art, or have a penchant for Louis XIV chairs, which certainly don't fit into the same box. Instead, build your own box, and fill it with things you love. Forgo any trendy design epithets, and instead slap a name tag on your box. After it's packed, your box will be beautifully brimming with visual representations of your travels, interests, favorite colors, and what makes you *happiest*.

LUXURY DESIGN

Before we get into budget, let's get into luxury. It's the sexier of the two terms anyway! I've already discussed the pitfalls of luxury interior design: We can't afford it, and we probably aren't friends with any upper-crust interior designers who can lend a helping hand—or provide a wholesale discount.

But what if we suspend our disbelief, just for a moment, and pretend. If we're striving for a luxury look, shouldn't we at least try to understand it? Prepare for an exercise in imagination.

Close your eyes. Oh wait, you can't. You have to read. Hmm. Well, take a deep breath instead. Maybe say "ommmm." Get ready to become someone else for an evening. Better yet, imagine not someone else—but yourself—in the following scenario:

Pretend you have a billion dollars in the bank. You drive a Rolls-Royce. Or, better yet, your driver chauffeurs you in your Rolls-Royce. That is, when he isn't sweeping you from party to party in your custom Aston Martin or your vintage Land Rover.

You pull up to your New York townhouse, which actually is three townhouses converted into one. This is just one of your many homes, the others being a Hamptons estate, a castle in the Scottish Highlands, and a modest sixteen-bedroom "flat" in London. You pause at your personal elevator and decide to do the healthy thing, walking up the marble stairs and through your foyer into a sprawling kitchen, which features two islands, three dishwashers, and a walk-in refrigerator.

To unwind, you enter the bathroom, which is impeccably clean thanks to your housekeeping team's hard work. You pour a sachet of dried roses into the bath, followed by a $200 tablespoon of French essential oil, custom-made for you during your shopping trip to Paris last month. The water runs smoothly from your Japanese tap, swirling into the basin below. You remember to close the solid-gold drain before too much of the oil slips away.

Your bathroom walls are coated in marble; one perfect, seamless slab. It was cut for you in Italy. Your designer sourced a piece with violet strains running throughout to complement the pale lavender walls in your adjacent bedroom. You laugh loudly and slowly, the way a rich person unabashedly tends to do, as you realize how greatly this marble must have increased your carbon footprint. But you're blissfully unaware of the logistics, as these mundane details were handled by your

An early sketch for my living room, in which I skimped on no luxurious details.

team, who had to source and custom-fit a private vessel to take it to America. And you don't even know this detail, but it cost $100,000 in bribes to the city for the contractors to hoist it up to the third story of the building by crane, violating more than fifty municipal codes. In fact, the traffic caused by the incident resulted in a nearby school canceling classes for the day.

But you relax, having no idea that this ever happened. Thank God your assistant knows to keep stressful situations to herself. You sink deeper into the warm water, and turn on the jets, which were completely bespoke: The vendor took a 3D scan of your body to identify your exact measurements and locations of any aches and pains you experience from your Tuesday-morning tennis lessons with Pierre.

You snap your fingers, and in walks Thomas, your butler. He's looking buffer than normal in his uniform. On a silver platter sits a tall glass of champagne. You forget the name of the champagne but remember it's one of 309 bottles your art adviser gave you as a Christmas thank-you. After all, you purchased the most expensive sculpture available on the Chinese market last year: 309 bottles represent the $309 million spent. Thomas, without saying a word, gives you a foot massage, then warms a towel for you over the Swedish coals in your en suite sauna.

You rise from the tub, confident and glowing from your recent diamond and ruby facial. Thomas cloaks you in the warm 800-thread-count-cotton towel mailed to you by a Saudi Arabian prince.

You stride with grace into your bedroom and admire the way candlelight is dancing across the gold-leaf ceiling. You don't know who lit the candles, but, like every night, they're lit. And, like every night, your bed has been turned down for the evening, Euro pillows tucked away somewhere—you have no idea where—and the comforter neatly pulled back, revealing silk sheets beneath. You're too tired to gua sha your face and decide to forgo your skin-care routine. Frankly, your skin looks perfect thanks to your aesthetician, Anya, and your lymphatic masseuse is coming tomorrow morning in lieu of an alarm. It's so nice to wake up to hands massaging your body and the sound of gongs amid mountain wind.

Your canopy-draped bed beckons your entry into a relaxing night of rich-person sleep. Because no matter how stressed you get, there's always a solution you can pay for. And stress is as bad for longevity as it is for your figure.

Snap snap! I hate to wake you from your dream, but unfortunately, I have to stop writing about it because I'm getting irrationally pissed that I'm not living in it either. And hey, aren't we supposed to be happy with what we have?? Gratitude, GRATITUDE!!! Be right back. I need to jot down three things I'm grateful for. Well, I guess I could just write it here, since I *am* writing anyway.

Okay. I'm grateful for . . . the fact that my dogs didn't poop inside today. It's only 10 A.M., though. Who knows what the day could hold?

That was one. Time for number two. Umm. I'm grateful that you actually read through my gratuitous rich person narrative without giving up on this book.

"Clare, why are you delusionally describing your life as an heiress. . . . Isn't this supposed to be a design guide?!" Indeed it is, dear reader, which brings me to my next point of gratitude! I'm grateful to rich people who hire designers with taste. No, really I am! I'm thankful to have the *inspiration* to design in an *aspirational* way. So, thank you, millionaires and billionaires, for your "inspiration donations" to this book.

In this section, I've sketched a few of my favorite luxury rooms created by world-renowned interior designers. With each depiction, I'll point out what aspects of the room make it look so damn *luxe.*

Mario Buatta, my favorite designer of all time, was called the "Prince of Chintz." Considered by many, including myself, the best American interior designer, he truly was an expert at creating transformative, luxurious, opulent spaces for his clients—who included the likes of Gloria Vanderbilt and Patricia Altschul (any Bravo fans reading?!).

His signature style was iconic, blending an appreciation for English country aesthetics with an American opulence marked by floral chintz fabrics, custom ornate drapery, and antique furniture. Buatta himself was a great collector of antiques, which is why each room he designed was infused with an elegant mix of expensive "clutter" that

Sketch of a living room designed by Mario Buatta

made it appear cozy and elevated. He was an expert at understanding good craftsmanship and had an eye for detail that went unmatched in his industry. When Buatta passed away in 2018, his estate was auctioned off at Sotheby's. The auction garnered more than $7 million as fans and design enthusiasts worldwide competed to win a piece of Mario's that they could call their own.

I could never pick a favorite room of his, but I think the example I sketched (see page 27) celebrates his spectacular eye for detail. Each surface is ornately cloaked, from the paneled wall to the occasional gingham-upholstered chair. Even the floor, which I'm sure was a beautiful old wood, wasn't forgotten. Mario had a Rolodex of highly skilled artisans at his beck and call, including architectural muralists, like the one who painted this geometric floor. He was never one to leave out texture. Take a look at the wicker chairs, which create contrast to the soft fabric of the sofa. A wrought-iron pendant adds historic roughness to the more demure upholstery fabric throughout the room.

Notice how symmetry rules this design: The sofa is flanked not only by identical chairs, but also by punctuating floor lamps. He was magically attuned to scale: Look at how the room is staged, tracing your eye from the low gingham chair in the foreground, up to the coffee table topiaries, to the sofa, floor lamps, and eventually the painting hung on the wall. He's created a visual diagonal from low to high, resulting in a pleasingly scaled room that feels "just right" to look at.

Collins Interiors is an interior design firm doing great work today. On the facing page I've sketched a cozy nook of their design. I want to call out a few custom details that make this room luxurious. If it weren't for the extravagance of detail and thoughtfulness, this room could look like a standard corner, but it feels delightful thanks to bespoke touches.

Let's start from the top: The ceiling is adorned with a flourish of faux bamboo, structured in a trellis shape. Beyond the ceiling, intricate paneling covers the walls, suggesting careful, considered design and craftsmanship. The sofa fits

I like to think that if you didn't know me, my house would tell you who I am.

Sketch of a sitting room
designed by Collins Interiors

Sketch of a bedroom designed by Bunny Williams

exactly in the room, making it clear that it was custom designed to fit within a millimeter of the close-cornered space. The Roman shades adorning both windows are also clearly custom, and they're a smart choice—no chunky curtain fabric takes up valuable floor space here. The room is decorated with a small, vertical row of plates hung on the wall. It's clear they aren't just your average dinnerware, but most likely expensive antiques that deserve to be displayed. Each surface is covered in its own custom treatment, from the overhead pendant lampshade fabric to the fringe at the bottom of the sofa. Together, all of these custom details *scream* luxury.

If Mario Buatta is the Prince of Chintz, Bunny Williams is the Empress of Elegance. Take this bedroom (opposite), which exudes luxury from every carefully curated surface. The four-poster bed is fit for a queen herself. It's clearly a one-of-a-kind piece. From the ornate inlays on the headboard to the scalloped curvature overtop, I've never quite seen anything like it, which feels *luxe* in part due to its *inaccessibility*. We also have another painted geometric wood floor, which feels wonderfully angular in comparison to the soft, billowy upholstery and cushions on the bed.

Everything down to the pillows, sporting Bunny's own monogram, is custom. The chair is clearly an antique, redone in a fabric that suits the room well.

These are all details that luxury interior designers consider before even starting to decorate a room. But they're details that we, as commoners, often overlook. So think carefully about the rooms in your home. What surfaces can you enhance with textile, paint, or decoration? What changes could you make in your home that would help you feel more like that billionaire in the bath?

INSTEAD OF SHOPPING ONLINE for cheap and trendy pieces, turn to your local antiques store. Whether your style is modern, eclectic, or even maximalist, you're sure to find a quality item that will add lots of character to your home.

BUDGET DESIGN

Yes, I preach about affordability, but I also refuse to skimp on quality for the sake of saving money. As I've established by now, I am all about budget. But I want to make an important clarification. *Budget* does not equal *cheap*. On my #BudgetLuxury journey, I've come to find that it's much smarter to buy an antique dresser than it is to buy a new one, no matter how low the price tag is. The difference is *quality*. They just don't make 'em like they used to. Furniture used to be handmade, ensuring longevity and durability with wood joinery, layers of thoughtful upholstery, and ornate detail. The craftsmanship was unique, featuring veneers of colorfully painted floral motifs or delicately turned table legs. Dresser drawers featured a plethora of panel variety, and always sported solid metal hardware. Have you ever opened an ancient desk drawer and noticed the dovetailed joints at each corner? Each piece of wood was cut specifically to fit another. Today? Open a modern drawer and the screws may just fall out.

Old furniture stands the test of time and, for some inexplicable reason, is more affordable than new furniture—which suffers in comparison to the quality of its predecessors. Newly made sofas are marketed in modern fonts that promise a happier home life (I know you can picture the ad—a well-dressed woman walks

This affordable antique chair in our nursery was upholstered in designer fabric. The pricetag definitely didn't reflect its value!

WHERE THE WILD THINGS
GUESS HOW MUCH I LOVE YOU
BABAR
FIRST
UMMER

into her sunlit living room, collapses onto a modern white couch, and joyfully cuddles with her Australian shepherd; what is she laughing at, anyway?). The reality of the big-box new couch is that after you've waited six to eight weeks and spent more than a thousand dollars, its arrival only harkens its swift and unavoidable departure. A cheaply made structure feels uncomfortable under your butt (a beautiful butt, which deserves better, okay?!). The sizing is strange—the seat is too deep for your feet to touch the ground, but your husband's legs are too long for the couch's short stature. And after your brother takes a post-dive-bar dive onto the cushions, which are bolstered by ill-equipped, flimsy springs, the couch is toast. It's only been eight months. Can you tell this is personal? My brother spent many nights on our couch in New York, waking up with back spasms and loud groans. So yes, I have fallen victim to Big Couch myself. But I found a better way.

Instead of getting hooked by targeted social media advertisements, I encourage you to check out your local Habitat for Humanity, Goodwill, or Facebook Marketplace for a well-made couch. Vintage furniture has already proven itself in the test of time; that two-hundred-year-old Chippendale hutch in your meemaw's living room is still standing for a reason! It's good quality. Unlike home furnishings of today, which are more often than not constructed of plastic, particleboard, or cheap metal, furniture used to be made to last! Some modern companies still make good-quality furniture, but they can be very expensive. And the new furniture that we can actually *afford* is mostly crap. Go the secondhand route. It's an affordable and smart approach.

On the Budget Luxury journey, you have to be brave. I need you to get over your fear of buying upholstered items secondhand. I did, and I wouldn't use *brave* as the first adjective to describe myself. *Resourceful,* definitely! And it was my resourcefulness that helped me conquer a lifelong fear of used couches, chairs, and other fabric items. Last summer, my mom and I were driving through a fancy town near my house and spotted an old couch on the side of the road. FREE read the sign thrown atop the tired cushions. My favorite word! So we pulled over to inspect the couch. Yes, the fabric was faded and the hems frayed, but this sofa was in great shape compared to other street sofas! It was a sleeper sofa with a queen mattress. I knew I'd struck gold when I lifted up the slipcover to find a beautiful chinoiserie pattern covering the original cushions.

Yet, I still hesitated. My mom and I went back and forth a bit, me expressing how gross it felt to take someone's couch. "Strangers slept on it! Pets sat on it! And . . . the FLUIDS?!" My mom, always the optimist, encouraged me to take it. She said she'd help me clean it, and that was that. I found myself driving the winding roads back to my house, my body totally contorted so that one hand could guide the steering wheel and the other could white-knuckle-grasp the edge of the couch, which was hanging halfway out of my trunk and conjuring up quite a few shocked facial expressions from the pedestrians we passed. I was terrified it'd slide out of my open trunk and into the car behind us, but we managed to pull into the driveway without a misdemeanor or a hospital bill.

We removed and washed the slipcover—twice. I hosed down the entire couch outside, scrubbing it with an extra-large brush and an entire bottle of cleaning solution. We aired out the inserts overnight, sprayed some Febreze, and swapped out the old mattress.

Just like that—I had an elegant, quality couch, free of cost! The #BudgetLuxury approach takes curiosity, risk, and resourcefulness. You'll need to be savvy when it comes to distinguishing cheap from budget-friendly, using *quality* as your guiding light to determine your design. Though you may spend some afternoons cursing me as you sweat through the process of sanding paint off an old table or nailing boards to your wall, I know you'll be so proud of your beautiful #BudgetLuxury home.

Sometimes, sticking to a budget takes a little imagination. These pillowcases were created by using a potato and some fabric paint!

ESSENTIAL TOOLS

I put this list of essential tools *before* the DIY guides for a reason: I don't want you to start a project without having the tools you need. Make sure that you've stocked up your toolbox, tool closet, tool bag, or tool shelf before taking on your next DIY. And here's why: There's nothing worse than realizing you don't own a pair of pliers when you're halfway through a nitty-gritty job. You're covered in dust, exhausted, but determined to finish by the day's end—and a trip to the store would take way too long! So you use your fingernails to pry out that bent nail. Ouch. See? I've been there, and I've learned from experience to make sure I've stocked up on the materials I need *before* getting wrapped up in creativity.

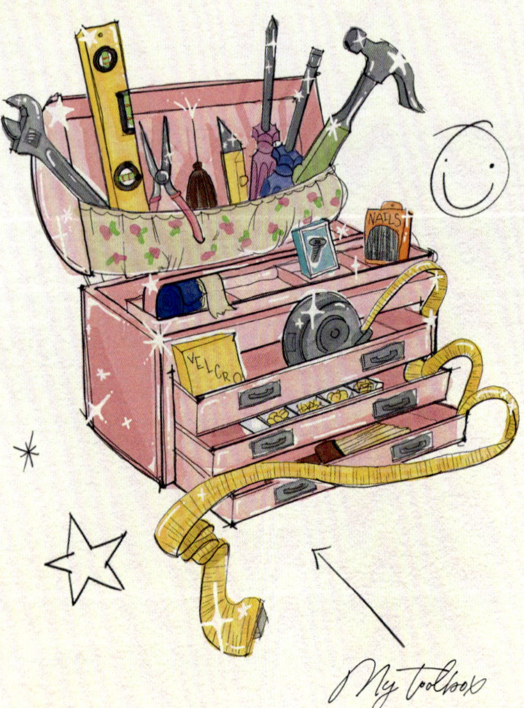

You don't need to spend hundreds of dollars before you take on your own Budget Luxury project. But I do have a list of tools you'll need if you're going to become a home improver like me. To save you money, I stuck to the bare necessities, and you probably already have a lot of these tools! I encourage you to review this list and check off what you already have before heading to the hardware store. I created a separate section of "optional" tools that are great to have, but not essential for your first few projects.

Remember, by taking on these projects yourself, you'll be saving thousands of dollars in the future. So invest *now* in quality tools that will help you for years to come. Fun fact: I inherited my Mimi's hammer. She had a set of essential tools that were FLORAL PRINT! So cute. If you can't find a floral-printed hammer, remember you can always paint it yourself. ;)

AWL: This pointy little tool allows you to create a small hole in your wall, which will hold a nail or screw in place and guide its way into the wall.

BOX SAW: I'm a bit queasy when it comes to using power saws. I prefer to make cuts on my box saw, which is relatively safe and easy to use. Just insert a piece of wood into the base and saw along the box's guides to cut a 45- or 90-degree angle.

DRILL: I use a Ryobi drill, since I like their battery system—I also have a Ryobi vacuum, speaker, nail gun, sander, etc.—and the batteries are all interchangeable. A drill is essential: It'll help you with hanging art, mounting shelves, hanging hooks, and general assembly. It also will make you feel very powerful.

GLOVES: Get a pair of leather or canvas work gloves. I use my gardening gloves when I'm working with rough materials. You should also have some rubber gloves on hand if you're working with anything toxic.

GLUE GUN: For crafting projects where I'm affixing small items, a glue gun is my go-to. Pick up a few bags of glue sticks as well, since you'll run through them fast!

HAMMER: For, well, nails.

LEVEL: This fascinating tool is my go-to for hanging art or shelves. No more squinting your eyes to see if a painting is crooked—the level will take care of that for you! Game changer: You can also use your phone! My mind was blown when I learned that iPhones come with a "level" feature.

MASKS: It's crucial that you protect your lungs while taking on these projects. I use 3M 8210 respirator masks when working with dust. If I'm working with any fumes, I prefer a respirator—the kind that looks straight out of the Apocalypse! I use the 3M P95 half-face respirator.

PAINT ROLLERS: The options available here are endless, so I'll simplify it. Buy what I use: Get a 9-inch roller frame and a few ¼ inch nap roller sleeves (the fuzzy cylinders that slide over the roller). I have found synthetic knit sleeves to be the best at retaining paint while also providing smooth coverage. The Purdy Marathon sleeves are unmatched for a smooth roll that lasts longest. An airtight case that keeps your roller cover from drying up is also handy to keep on hand. The last thing you'll need is an extension rod for reaching the top of your walls and ceilings.

PAINT MIXERS: When you buy your paint, ask the salesperson to throw in a few extra paint mixers. They come in handy if you save leftover paint and need to mix it up later down the line. Another freebie you can get from the paint store is a paint can opener!

PAINT TRAY: Get a sturdy plastic paint rolling tray. To make cleanup easier, I use the cheap plastic inserts to line the tray. But if you're really ballin' on a budget? Saran Wrap does a great job, too. Oh, you like my cheap hacks?! Grab a disposable pie tin from your pantry instead of buying a paint tray.

Clare's Mom Says:

Sure, you could BUY an extension pole, but check the broom closet first. Did you know that most household brooms unscrew from their broomstick? And like magic, most paint roller frames screw perfectly onto the end of a broomstick!

PAINTBRUSHES: Get an XL flat brush for large wall sections, an angled sash brush for cutting corners and molding, and a 1- to 2-inch round brush for painting furniture and applying finishes. Synthetic bristles are superior. I use Purdy nylon and polyester blend brushes.

PAINTER'S TAPE: Creates crisp, clean lines and protects unpainted surfaces from paint splashes and unsteady strokes. The only type you should be purchasing is the blue FrogTape Pro Grade Painter's Tape. Nothing else compares!

PICTURE-HANGING KIT: If I'm hanging items heavier than 3 pounds, I appreciate the added safety of a hook instead of a bare nail. Buy a kit that includes nails of all sizes and different kinds of hooks. I think people tend to use too-big nails for most hanging jobs. To avoid completely ruining your walls, your kit should have a guide to help you pick and choose your nail size according to the weight of the item you're hanging.

PLIERS: You'll need a tool to help you bend wire, pull out old screws, and essentially act as an indestructable robot hand. I have a pair of needlenose pliers, and those work well for my purposes!

PRY BAR: This tool is essential for any "demo" project. You can use it to rip off molding, unearth tiles, or pry off anything you can't grasp with your hands.

PUTTY KNIFE: I have a few different sizes of these. A large metal putty knife helps you spread joint compound across a wall, while a plastic one helps smooth out wallpaper bubbles. A small, rigid putty knife is great for chipping off old paint or applying caulk to holes in the wall.

SAFETY GLASSES: Make sure you wear these when doing any demolition, sanding, or sawing. Trust me, sawdust in your eyes isn't fun.

SANDERS: Pick up a hand sander for light sanding jobs like tabletops and bureaus, and an electric orbital sander for bigger jobs, like removing paint or smoothing out jagged surfaces.

SANDPAPER: Make sure you have a variety of "grits" for your sandpaper. The higher the grit number, the finer the sanding job. An 80-grit sandpaper is very rough and good for muscling through tough jobs, like paint removal. As your sanding progresses, move up in grit; for example, if you used 80-grit to get through sanding paint off a shelf, move to a 120-grit to smooth the wood. For your final pass, use a 220-grit on the wood to ensure a smooth, non-damaging sand job.

SCISSORS: Get a nice pair of fabric scissors, preferably all-metal. They should glide easily through fabric without creating a frayed edge.

SCREWDRIVERS: You should have a standard size Phillip's head as well as a flathead screwdriver. I have an all-in-one screwdriver, which is great because it has multiple sizes of each head style.

STAPLE GUN: This tool is a necessity for taking on upholstery projects of your own. Instead of using messy glue or expertly sewing, a staple gun gets the job done quickly, and permanently.

STUD FINDER: A battery-operated stud finder is good when you're hanging a heavy piece of art or shelving. Drywall isn't a strong anchor for heavy items, but with a stud finder, you can locate beams in your walls, which provide a stronger hold for hanging weighty items.

TAPE MEASURE: Though I have a high-tech interior design laser measure, I tend to forgo it in favor of the good old dependable metal one. You'll need one of these for hanging art, measuring your living area before thrifting furniture, and taking on tasks like wallpapering and rug selection. Make sure you have one that's long and can measure spaces up to 20 feet.

UTILITY KNIFE: I love mine. The utility knife, or box cutter, is sturdier than an X-Acto knife. It's great for cutting heavier materials than paper, but it still possesses the delicate integrity of a smaller knife when it comes to cutting wallpaper or crafting. Pick up a set of replacement razor blades as well, so that you're ready to swap them out when your knife gets dull.

VELCRO HANGERS: If you rent, or tend to switch up your space a lot, Velcro hangers are a great option for temporarily affixing decor to the wall. To stretch my dollar, I cut up Command Velcro strips into multiples.

WRENCH: A wrench has lots of good uses: fastening, tightening, and, most helpful, removing stripped screws. Buy an adjustable wrench, which can help you loosen bolts of any size!

OPTIONAL, BUT BENEFICIAL

HEAT GUN: If you're restoring your home, or old furniture, a heat gun is great for removing multiple layers of paint. Aim the gun at the paint, watch it bubble up, then scrape it away with a putty knife!

KNEEPADS: When I was pregnant, I finally caved and ordered a pair of these. I was on day three of working on a bathroom floor, moaning and groaning through the project, when I decided that my joints were no longer those of an eighteen-year-old lacrosse player. And, boy, were my knees happy to have a bit of extra cushioning while working. A gardening pad can work for this purpose, too.

NAIL GUN: This is very useful for projects that involve lots and lots of nails. While a hammer and nail are sufficient for hanging up art, a nail gun is much more suitable for bigger projects that require multiple lines of nails in a row. I use it to install paneling. Instead of tediously hammering each nail in, which can then cause damage to the wood if you miss a swing, the nail gun is a swift, efficient, and consistent way to fasten things together!

PAINTER'S PLASTIC: I use these plastic sheets to cover furniture when I'm painting. You can cover your whole floor to protect it from drips. I even use it when I'm not painting—for example, I was sanding in my husband's office, which doesn't have a door, and I didn't want the dust to spread to the rest of the house, so I taped plastic over the doorway to ensure all toxins were sealed away.

SHOP-VAC: If you're doing a lot of sanding and anticipate that your project will create dust, I recommend having a Shop-Vac. Not all vacuums are created equal, and my household vacuum wouldn't be capable of sucking up demo debris and wet messes.

CHAPTER 1

TECHNIQUES

PLANNING YOUR PROJECT

I'm about to walk you through the very simple, tried-and-true planning method that I use before jumping into the creative process of ordering wallpaper, buying paint, or sourcing furniture. It may not be as sophisticated as a "real" interior designer's approach, but it does the job, and you'll be fully capable of trying it yourself! Once I finish my planning process, I'm fully equipped to dive into my project headfirst. This process consists of three parts: making a floor plan, mood boarding, and creating a budget.

I'm not a big rule follower, and while I hope you take most of my advice loosely, I do insist that you at least follow the order of these three parts. It's important to start with a floor plan so that while mood boarding, you know what items to look out for. And once you get to budgeting, your mood board and floor plan will prove to be necessary references as you compile an all-encompassing list of each item to determine the overall budget.

With a thorough plan in your back pocket, you'll feel less like a chicken with its head cut off when you run into an obstacle in your project. You'll be able to adjust accordingly, refer to your plans, and make informed budgeting decisions that you feel comfortable with.

Making a Floor Plan

Before you start buying the cherry-on-top decor items like curtains and art, you need to make a plan. A floor plan! When you sketch out a plan for your room, you can look at your space from an accurate perspective and figure out the best way to fill it. Your plan will tell you how wide your curtains should be, what size rug will realistically fit under the bed, or even help you maximize space that potentially could have gone unnoticed. By scaling the room down onto a small, digestible, two-dimensional piece of paper, you can study it from the matter-of-fact perspective of a scientist, instead of viewing it as you do daily, from your own biased perspective.

Before I studied design, I had no idea how to draw a room. Looking back at my sketches, I admittedly cringe a little bit. They looked so juvenile! The most glaring issue was that I had no comprehension of scale, so a bedside table might look terribly minuscule compared to the mammoth lamp I had drawn sitting atop it.

I've made strides in my sketching techniques, which is great for illustrating a fun book, but when it comes to planning a design, don't worry: These skills aren't necessary. I'm not going to teach you how to *draw*. In fact, you don't actually need artistic skills to create a floor plan.

Drawing to scale sounded intimidating to me at first. Remember when I told you I couldn't do math? Yeah, so converting 18 feet to a ¾ inch scale wasn't the easiest thing for me to do in grad school. But the beautiful thing about scale is that you can create your own. And to make it easy, I always go for a 1:1 ratio. With this method, one square on my graph paper represents one foot. So, if I know my wall is 8 feet wide, all I have to do is draw a line across 8 squares! It's *that simple.*

Although I love to visualize a room by sketching it out, in this section I'll teach you how to plan a space the easy way—no artistic talent needed.

Scaled Furniture

Copy my bird's-eye sketches to create your own floor plan!
(Scale: one foot = one square.)

The How-To

MATERIALS

Graph paper

A good black pen
(I love Sharpie S-Gels in the .5 size)

A few markers for shading

1. With your tape measure, measure the boundaries of your room.
2. Start in a corner and measure to the next corner, doorframe, or window. Jot that length down to remember it.
3. Now take that measurement and draw it onto the graph paper. Remember, one foot = one square. Say you measured 5 feet from the corner of the room to a window: Draw a line 5 squares long. (If you have extra inches in your measurement, use your best estimate of length.)
4. Continue measuring around the room and drawing corresponding lines on your paper.
5. Eventually, you'll be right back at the corner where you started. If you've measured and recorded correctly, your last line should meet up with your starting point.
6. I draw my furniture icons at the same scale, then cut them out with scissors. You can then play with where your furniture will go by sliding the cutouts around the plan!
7. Once you've decided how you'd like to arrange your room, tape down the cutouts.

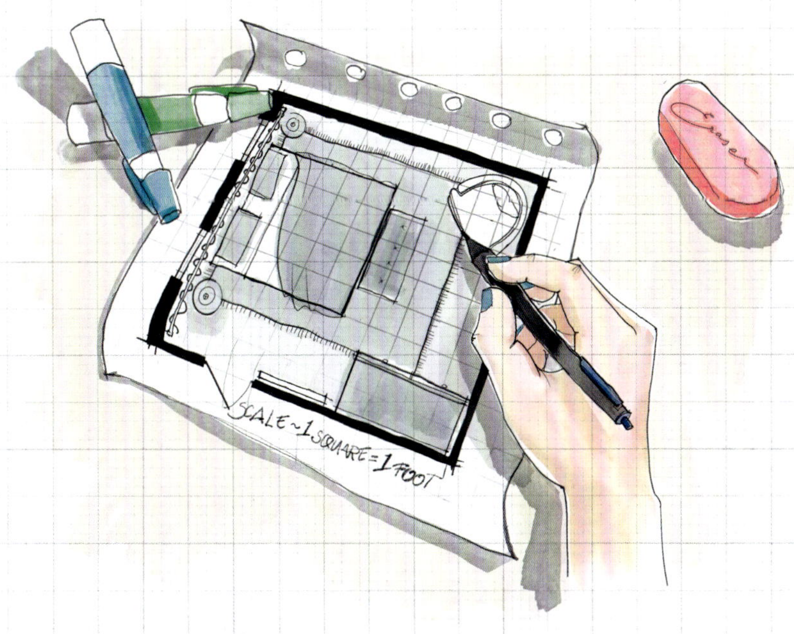

build with ferguson
bellevue abstract pendant
Bed Bath & Beyond Erin Gates Rug

Mood Boarding

When it comes to envisioning your room, it helps to identify examples of styles you like. Remember how fun it was to cut images out of magazines to create colorful collages when you were little? For me, this hobby never died.

I don't throw away magazines—*especially not design magazines,* as you can always source inspiration from them. It's fun to see what rooms have aged terribly, and which ones still look timeless, when leafing through an *Architectural Digest* from ten years ago. Observing the past through design photographs helps you understand the ingredients to a timeless room—toile fabric, airy tones, antique wood furniture . . . the list goes on! Recently I ordered a stack of vintage *Martha Stewart Living* copies off eBay. I love looking through her old ideas and dog-earing projects that would be fun to try.

Sites like Pinterest are great for finding inspiration. However, if you're starting from scratch and don't know which phrases to use when searching for inspiration, the old-fashioned way is best.

Cut out anything you're gravitating toward—even images from advertisements are fair game. If you find a page with a chair you love, but you dislike the room it's in, cut out just the chair!

Grab a big poster board, or even a blank wall, and tape your favorite images onto it. Consider your images with an inquisitive mind. What qualities do they share? Is there a color palette beginning to take shape? What sorts of patterns are you drawn to? Are the rooms minimalist or maximalist?

Tape your floor plan onto your board next to your collage. This way, you can connect the dots between inspiration and actuality, drawing connections between the aesthetic you want to achieve and the physical room where you'll achieve it.

As you move through your project, you'll continue adding to your mood board. Add fabric swatches, paint samples, and printouts of furniture and decor you've selected. You can get creative with how you make your board—for my kitchen mood board, I used thumbtacks to secure a tile sample. By now, your mood board will look a lot more "professional interior designer" than "third-grade collage enthusiast." Hang up your mood board where you'll see it often, and, by the way—use tape that's easy to remove. You may just find a better idea tomorrow! Good design is all about ideation—reworking your ideas can only improve them.

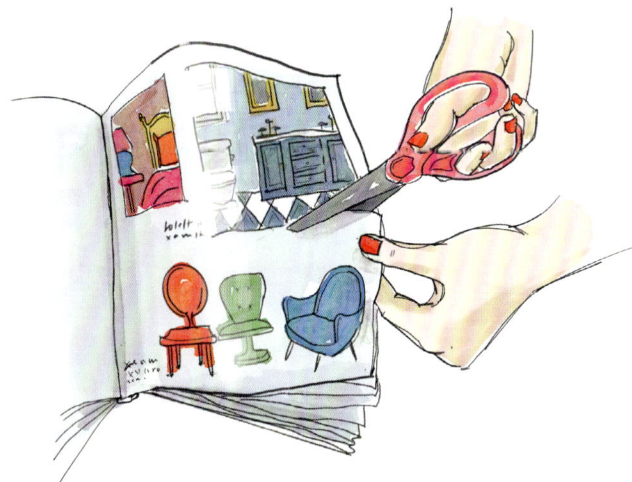

Creating a Budget

Money. Nobody likes to talk about it. I, honestly, don't like to even think about it! But I've come to really enjoy the process of *saving* it. At its core, this book is about learning how to create beautiful interiors without breaking the bank. But without a plan, it's easy to run off course. A budgeting plan is useful not only for saving money, but also to list exactly what you're going to need for each project.

What does an heiress with millions of dollars have in common with a broke recent college grad? The capability to decorate their home *atrociously*. Without a plan, they're both just as capable of creating something . . . *ugly*. Whew! That's the first time I've used that word in my book. It's an ugly word. Oh, jeez. That's now the second time I've used the word *ugly*. OMG, we're at three! But in all seriousness, it's a mean word, and I don't like to use it. It feels like a swear to me; as someone who lives and breathes aesthetics, it's a word I never want to encounter in my own work.

Everyone has their own taste, and your taste may be completely different from mine. That doesn't mean I would find your home *ugly*. To me, ugliness in interior design stems from insecurity. But now that I've taught you to throw your insecurities to the wind and embrace your personal style, you'll be much better equipped to create a home that feels beautiful to *you* and will be respected by those around you who can see *you* in each pillow, color scheme, or paint color.

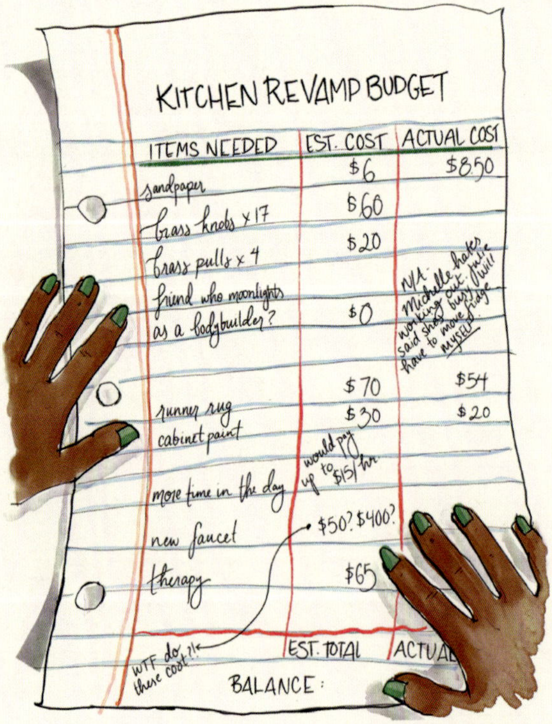

BUDGETING TIPS

HAVE A PLAN: The next step is to plan. Planning will help you settle on a design style, give you a timeline, and identify what factors you may not have considered yet. Planning will also help you stay on track with your spending, which you'll thank yourself for in the long run. It's easy to go over the edge financially when it comes to home improvement. With your plan, you can reassess your budgeting mistakes at any time or take advantage of savings: You'll have the foresight to know that, for example, if you save on the cost of wallpaper by purchasing secondhand, you'll have enough budget left over to hire a pro to hang your wallpaper, which could save you lots of time.

BUDGET YOUR EMOTIONS: Overspending can lead to big-time emotions, and emotions can create a slippery slope that usually lands you in one dreaded spot: that area between a rock and a hard place. But if you have a plan, you can save yourself some distress when these situations eventually occur, because you have a clear view of your many options.

PICK YOUR PRICE: To begin planning your budget, decide how much you can spend. Though I am very nosy, I can't actually look at your bank account. Unfortunately, that's your job. And though it can be scary to evaluate your budget, think of what you'll save if you stick to your plan! Designing with a budget in mind is a proven way to spend less money than haphazardly putting a room together over time, splurging sporadically on furniture and hiring professionals to do the job for you.

INCENTIVIZE SAVING: If you're extremely turned off by thinking about money: try motivating yourself with an incentive. Estimate the monetary difference between taking a #BudgetLuxury approach and taking an approach without a plan. If you stick to your budget, what do you have left over? What can you get as a little treat with some of that money you saved?

ITEMIZE YOUR BUDGET: Once you've written down your maximum budget, you need to figure out how that money will be dispersed across your project. Start listing what you need. It's obvious that you'll write down chairs, rugs, sofas . . . but what about DIY projects, or hiring a professional to hang your TV? Make sure that you include each item you'll need, including tools and services.

TIME IS MONEY: Listing all materials needed is a helpful way to plan your timeline, as well as your budget. If you order some of these items online, their arrival time determines when you can start. On a separate piece of paper, write out a realistic timeline with the goal end date being one you feel confident in reaching.

DELEGATING COSTS: Now that you have a list of all products you need for your project, start weighing the importance of each as well as the estimated cost. I often divide my total number by four. With four smaller numbers, it's easier to assign anticipated cost to four categories.

LET'S LOOK AT AN EXAMPLE PROJECT: I wanted to transform my guest room into a dual use closet/guest room. I gave myself a budget of $700. Next, I split my budget up in four parts: **1)** tools **2)** furniture **3)** decor **4)** fixtures. This gave me $175 to spend on each category. As you can see in the pictured budget document, some categories will require more spending than others. Check out how I carry the remainder from one project over to another, and also track deficits.

- My total estimated budget was $620, meaning I still had $80 to work with before I maxed out at $700.
- To determine how to shift your budget around, take a look at your other categories. Where are you over budget? Under budget?
- I went over budget on furniture, and under on every other category. To even out the playing field, I needed to split up my remaining $80. I put $40 toward buying a nicer rug. I added one more shoe storage unit for $20, and tacked the last $20 on to the paintbrushes, which allowed me to buy ones with nicer bristles!

ALWAYS SAVE YOUR RECEIPTS: Now that you've listed your items and added a column for estimated cost, add one more column where you'll record the actual price you paid. With easy-to-google prices like wallpaper or tools, these numbers should match up well.

ADJUST ACCORDINGLY: There's a good reason for price variables—furniture spans a vast cost differential! For example, in my guest room project I was looking for a vintage ottoman. I'd estimated that would cost $100, and, boy, was I wrong. The one I found was double that price, but it was the perfect size and color for the room. When you find yourself in my shoes, take a deep breath, it's *okay*! Just go through your list and decide what items you can spend less on to make up for your splurge—maybe you can look for a less expensive lamp, or paint your old side tables instead of purchasing new ones. In my case, I decided to use my own childhood dresser instead of purchasing a new one, saving well over $200.

NOBODY'S PERFECT: As you journey through your design project, take note of budgeting errors and mishaps you encounter. On a positive note, perhaps you've found new ways to save, like borrowing your neighbor's ladder instead of buying one from Home Depot (do you even have room in your house for that, btw?!). Or maybe you went overboard on buying new tools because you were just. so. excited. Been there! Learn from this project in order to make your next one run smoother. You'll learn about your design priorities. You may find yourself flexible when it comes to some aspects of your budget, but rigid when it comes to other costs.

REFLECT LATER: Save your budgeting documents in a folder and look back on them after time has passed. What decisions stood the test of time? Were there any products or ideas that didn't work out? Maybe skimping on purchasing a rug pad was good for your wallet, but bad for your back after slipping a few too many times on an unanchored rug.

TOTAL BUDGET: $700

TOOLS	**budget $175**
New paintbrushes	est. $15
Drop cloth	est. $10
Paint—1 qt pink	est. $30
Paint—1 qt green	est. $30
Paint—1 gallon light pink	est. $30
TOTAL	est. **$115**
Remainder	+$60

FURNITURE	**budget $175**
Dresser	est. $200
Ottoman	est. $100
TOTAL	est. **$300**
Remainder	-$125

DECOR	**budget $175**
Large Rug	est. $80
Small Rug	est. $40
Wall mirror	est. $20
TOTAL	est. **$140**
Remainder	+$35

FIXTURES	**budget $175**
Rolling Rack x3	est. $45
Shoe storage	est. $20
TOTAL	est. **$65**
Remainder	+$110

PAINT LIKE A PRO

The most crucial part of executing a beautiful paint job actually isn't the act of painting. In my opinion, it's the part where you pick your color. This can be daunting for some, and I used to hate picking colors. I always worried that I'd pick the wrong color. And that certainly happened many times. There was a year of my life where I had to repaint the same room THREE times because I just couldn't get it right. Where I went wrong was giving in to my impulsivity. Instead of sampling real paint on my wall, I'd pick a color from a card at the store, bring it home, and decide—based off a teeny tiny piece of paper instead of the actual paint! . . . I shudder looking back at this! What was I thinking?! Learn from my mistakes and pick your paint in a cool, calm, collected, and PATIENT state of mind. Stick to my rules, and you'll be much less likely to regret your paint color choice. And remember, everything is fixable—if you *really* don't like your color, you can always paint over it. You might be swearing under your breath the whole time, but throw on an angry playlist and make the best of it.

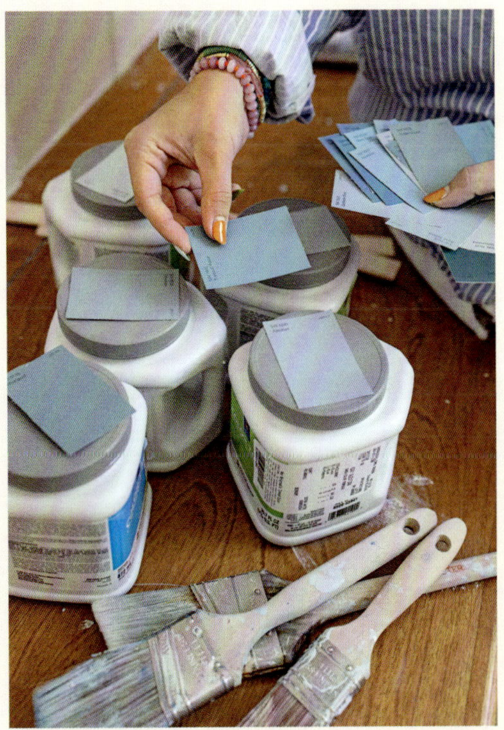

OPPOSITE: For thin areas like between these panels, I'm using a brush to put on the first coat. **ABOVE LEFT:** After sifting through dozens of blue paint chips, I took home a selection of sample pots to try on the wall. **ABOVE RIGHT:** Getting ready to paint sample swatches on the wall.

Selecting Your Color

Those little paint chips you can take home for free from the paint shop are fun. They're useful for mood boarding and learning which colors you're leaning toward when you begin a project. But that's about where their virtue ends. Countless times, I've bought a paint color after liking it on a chip. And countless times, I've been let down by the final coat—it *never* looks the same as it does on the chip. This is because the finish on the card tends to be much flatter than your actual paint, and often it's a digitally printed rendering of the color, which can't possibly replicate the real thing. Instead of getting chips, do some online research and write down a list of colors you'd like to *sample*.

Remember that the paint colors you see photographed in beautiful rooms from magazines and blog posts aren't representative of their real-life tone. Paint colors change with photo editing and printing, and everyone's lighting is different. Your favorite influencer may have a beautiful, calming sage-green bathroom, but when you try the color in your home, it looks like the wall got puked on! Don't be tempted to choose a paint color that reads light and airy in a magazine spread, as your own home may be lacking in natural light in comparison. For this reason, I'm not going to list my "favorite" "go-to" paint colors. Sure, I've bought paint after seeing a beautiful color in a blog post, and sometimes it works out, but I recommend choosing your own.

I find that in a small chip, colors don't appear as bright or overwhelming as they could on your walls. A bright green on a little chip may look subtle, but when you blow it up times one thousand, it may appear jarringly neon on your walls! When in doubt, pick a color that's

LEFT: Swatching a variety of blue tones.

OPPOSITE: Large samples provide a better visual than small swatches, but the best method is to sample the real paint on your wall.

Clare Rule
Before covering your entire wall, always sample a small swatch of color first to make sure you love it!

toned down a few shades from the highly saturated one you're drawn to. It takes a bold person to live with bold colors, and if you're drawn to them—go for it! But for me, it's more realistic to choose wall colors that will provide a muted, tonal backdrop to more colorful decor.

At the hardware store, ask for paint samples of each color you're interested in, so that you can take them home and paint them onto your walls. Make sure you paint two coats, practicing patience to let each coat dry, since one coat won't be a true representation of the color.

Once you've brushed some sample tones onto your wall, visit them throughout the day. In the evening, you'll notice the colors appear much warmer than they did in the morning. Artificial lighting reflects a much different shade than natural light does. Ask yourself when you'll be in the room most—morning? afternoon? Select a color you love in *all* lights, but make sure it looks beautiful at the time of day you'll be spending the most time in the room. What about the usage of the room—is it a breakfast nook? You may want a color that feels invigorating, to kick you off on a happy foot in the morning, like green or yellow. An office wall? How about a Zen blue to help you calm down after dealing with your asshole coworkers? Your bedroom, where you need to unwind after dealing with said coworkers, should feel like a comforting hug—a romantic pale pink, perhaps?

Maybe you want a blank slate in your entire home. I've seen gorgeous houses swathed in all white. And white is certainly not a basic color—there are thousands of white variants to choose from! If you're looking to complement your white walls with subtle contrast, consider a darker- or lighter-toned white for your trim. Or paint the trim the same white as your walls! Remember, it's up to you to decide, and I know you're capable. I'm just here to help the process run smoothly.

Don't forget about your ceiling, the so-called fifth wall. This year I took the pink wall color in my guest room and carried it up onto the ceiling, and though my arms ached after doing so, I was so happy I did. Painting the ceiling totally transformed the room. I was so enamored with the look that I went on to paint my bedroom ceiling in a high-gloss finish. The result was beautiful—at night, the ceiling reflects my lamplight back down into the room, creating an ethereal, relaxing atmosphere. I love the ceiling-paint approach for bedrooms; it feels like being wrapped up in a comforting hug of color.

OPPOSITE: After some deliberation over samples, I went with this briny and complicated blue tone.

Finishes: A "Primer"

After you've chosen the perfect color, you're not out of the woods yet! It's important that you select the proper finish for your job. Don't be overwhelmed by the differences between finishes. Take a look at my guide, and you'll have an easier time making a decision:

HIGH-GLOSS: This sparkling, highly reflective finish is a go-to for special areas you want to emphasize, like decorative trim, kitchen cabinets, and furniture. It's especially beautiful when hit by sunlight but also lovely at nighttime, when it captures even the slightest dancing glow from nearby lamps. While high-gloss is without a doubt my favorite paint finish, I'm unable to drench my entire home with it, thanks to one drawback: It shows off any and all imperfections. While optically mesmerizing, the reflective characteristic of this finish highlights flaws. You're likely to have more than a few imperfections on a big wall, from nail holes to basic wear and tear, so high-gloss isn't the best choice for larger spaces. Plus, parents be warned: High-gloss is especially vulnerable to grubby little fingerprints.

SEMI-GLOSS: If you knock high-gloss down a few notches from A-list to C-list celeb, you're looking at semi-gloss. While it isn't as shiny as high-gloss, it does reflect light and conceals inconsistencies better than high-gloss. Because it's easy to wipe down, this finish is great for areas that see more wear and tear, like baseboards, bathrooms, kitchens, and hallways.

SATIN: Satin has a subtle sheen, though it isn't reflective or shiny. Satin is my go-to for bedrooms and living rooms. It reflects a subtle amount of light, which makes each wall glow in a varying shade of your color. To me, satin feels cozy. I love the warm glow of my bedroom at night, as my lamps cast a golden tone against the green satin paint.

EGGSHELL: Less reflective than satin, but not as dull as matte, eggshell is a finish that works wonderfully on older walls. If you have areas of your home where you don't want to highlight imperfections, eggshell is your best bet. With eggshell, your paint will fall back, allowing other decor in the room to stand out. Keep in mind that the tone of your color may appear more muted due to the flat-finish quality.

MATTE: At the bottom of the shine-spectrum, we have matte. This finish reflects *no* light, absorbing it instead. Who knew you'd be getting a science lesson today?! I wouldn't consider using matte in a home with kids or dogs. It's very easy to ding up and very hard to clean. Matte is often used in museums; the Guggenheim's galleries are coated in a matte white paint—which allows the artwork to stand out. So if you're looking for a mature, understated paint, matte is perfect for you. If you have a gorgeous semi-gloss painted fireplace mantel that you want to emphasize, consider flanking its adjacent walls in matte finish. Or if you're planning a gallery wall of your favorite art, matte creates a nice contrast against the high reflectivity of glass frames.

HIGH-GLOSS
SEMI-GLOSS
SATIN
EGGSHELL
MATTE

Painting a Room: The Basics

The most dramatic, simple way to completely change the look of a room is with paint. Interior painting is time consuming, but it certainly isn't reserved for professionals. I've painted at least twenty rooms at this point in my life, and if you don't count the lime-green stripes on my bedroom wall in high school, I'm usually pretty thrilled with how paint can elevate a room. When it comes to painting a room, of course it'll be easier if you can get a friend or loved one to help. But I take on most painting projects solo. I have my friend the ladder, and my pal the extra-long roller extension. It's exhaustive yet highly satisfying work, and by the end of a day of painting, I feel super proud looking at myself in the mirror. Make sure you have fun with it. I always play music or listen to a true-crime podcast to help me through a long day of rolling color onto walls. I've noticed a few times while painting walls that my mind feels clear for the first time in months. There's something about the combination of straining physical labor with the repetitive motion of rolling the paint that gets me into a meditative zone. So grab your ex-boyfriend's stupid college shirt, a pair of old jeans, and get ready to destroy your outfit with paint smears and spatters. If you stick to these guidelines, you'll be perfectly capable of achieving a professional look.

OPPOSITE: In my bedroom, I chose the "color drenching" technique, where each surface is coated with the same color—even the ceiling!

Special thanks to Kamil Jankowski at KJ Global painting, who helped me tackle major painting projects while I was pregnant!

The How-To

SET THE SCENE

1. Lay down a drop cloth or old sheet (**A**) to ensure your floors stay clean.
2. Remove any outlet covers and cover the plugs with painter's tape (**B**).
3. Sand any irregular wall patches, and caulk over any holes.
4. Open up windows to get proper ventilation in the room.
5. Tape around all edges in straight lines (**C**, **D**). To achieve a perfectly straight tape border, don't push the tape down as you go. Instead, tape down one end, then stretch the tape all the way out to its end point. Stick the end point on, smoothing from one end of the tape to the other.

PREPPING YOUR PAINT

1. Before pouring paint into your tray, make sure to thoroughly mix it (**A**). This ensures that the consistency and color are correct.
2. Pour enough paint to coat your entire tray (**B**).

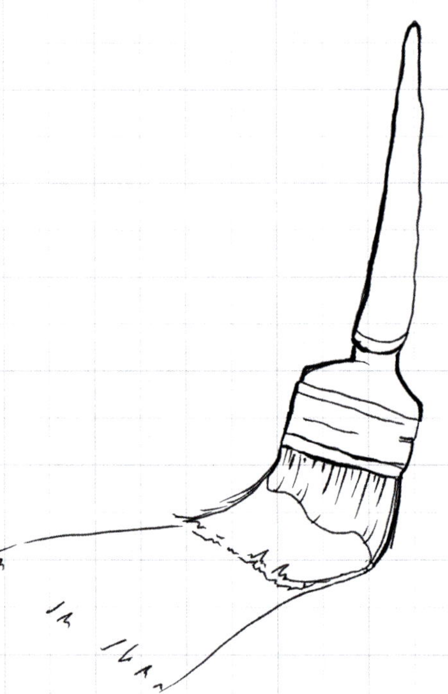

Set the Scene

A

B

C

D

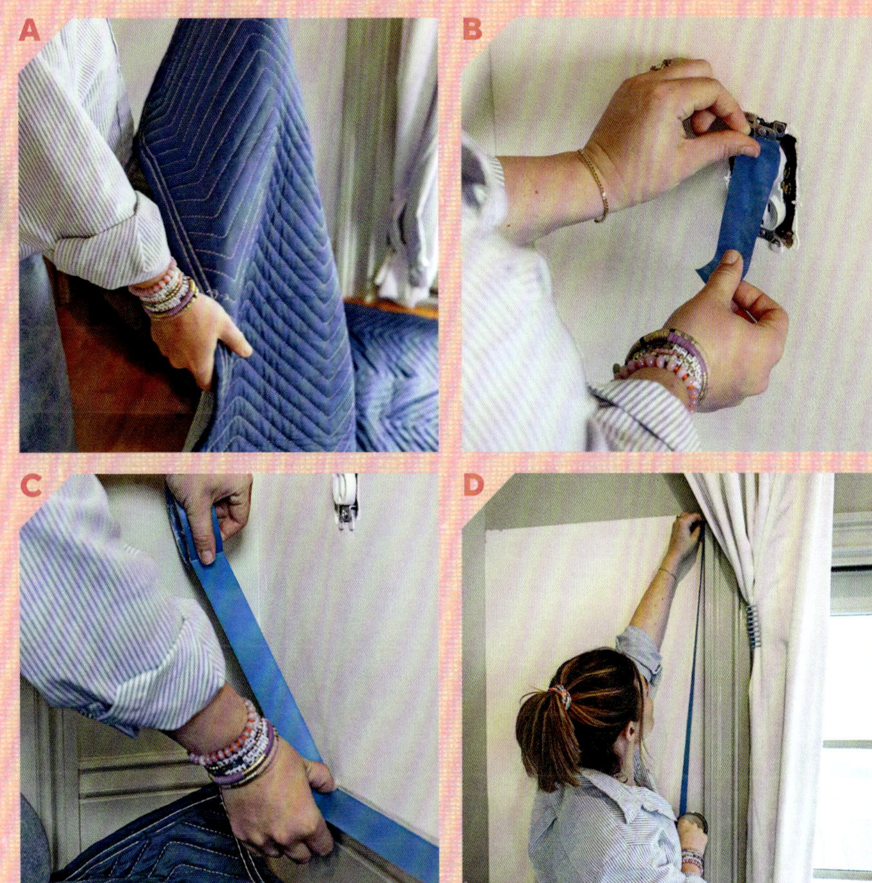

Prepping Your Paint

A

B

PAINTING

1. Before rolling the paint, you are going to "edge out" the wall with a paintbrush. In even, smooth strokes, cover the edges and corners with about 6 inches of paint (**A**). The paintbrush border creates a neat edge at the top and bottom of your wall, plus, with a brush, you're able to paint tough areas like corners and crevices that the roller wouldn't be able to fit into (**B**).
2. Coat your roller with paint. It should be covered, but not dripping (**C**).
3. Roll your paint onto the wall (**D**), reloading often to make sure you're painting a consistent coat. You can tell the roller is too wet if you notice bubbles or dripping on the wall.

Clare Tip

Some companies make special formulas of paint that only require one coat. They're often more expensive, but save lots of time.

4. Once the first coat is on, follow the can's directions on dry time. I usually become impatient: When it's dry to the touch (after about two or three hours), I start on my second coat.
5. When you've painted the second coat, wait for it to dry to evaluate whether you'll need a third round of painting. Often you will!
6. To paint trim, use a brush. I like using a higher gloss for the trim, which creates a shiny contrast to the more matte wall finish. Follow the same preparation, taping underneath the trim and on the ceiling above to ensure a clean line. You'll likely need only two coats here!

RECIPE

FROM THE KITCHEN OF: *Clare Sullivan*

Taking care of your brushes is crucial! Never let them sit in water for more than an hour, and definitely don't leave them covered in paint. If you do forget to wash your brushes thoroughly, here's a great tactic for cleaning even the cakiest of paintbrushes: Boil a pot of white vinegar, then soak your brushes in the hot liquid for a few hours. Brush through the bristles with a wire brush or fork to clean up any remaining dried paint.

A
B
C
D

WALLPAPERING

I fell in love with wallpaper after trying my first peel-and-stick project. Of course there were some frustrating moments: Wallpaper is sticky, and if you lack vigilance, it can suddenly be stuck to you, to the wall, to your ladder, and worst of all—to *itself*! That's the last thing you want, as it's nearly impossible to pull the adhesive side of two pieces apart without damaging your design. But once I got the hang of hanging wallpaper, I was sold. There's no better way to inject your room with color, pattern, and personality!

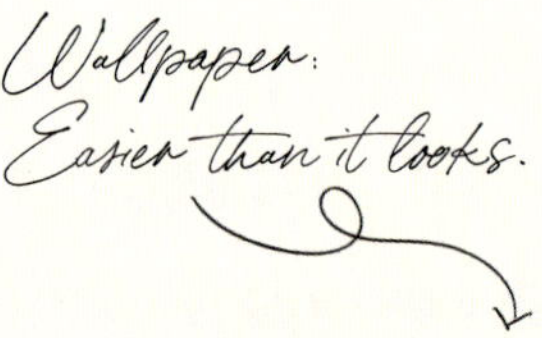

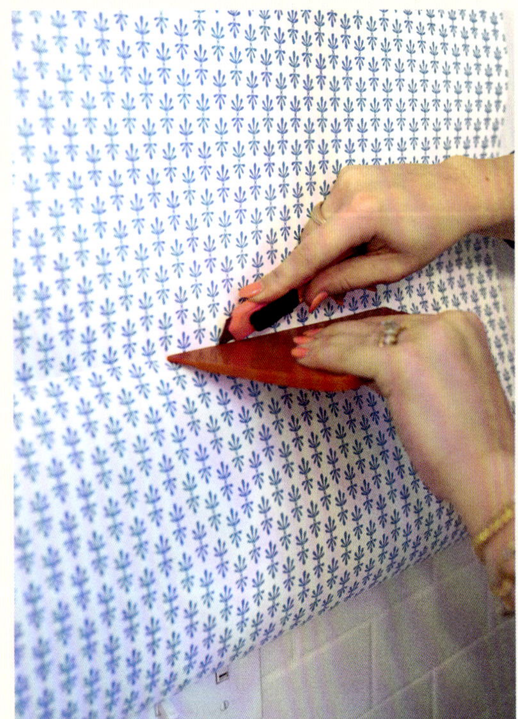

EN
BABAR
À PARIS
BABY'S JOURNAL
GOODNIGHT MOON
Where's the Puffin?
Silverstein Falling Up

Thank
Heaven For
Little Boys

Wallpaper

While paint is an excellent backdrop for your room, wallpaper is more than that—it's the shining star. If you really want to make your mark, and create a home that feels like you, I encourage you to find wallpaper you love. It's great for setting a mood. Want your closet to feel glamorous and chic? Try an elevated animal print. You're hoping to add texture and warmth to your living room? A colored grass cloth works wonders. Moreover, wallpaper exudes luxury in its very essence. See, most people are intimidated by it. You may think you'd mess it up, or it'd be too hard to do by yourself. But if you think wallpaper is reserved for the seasoned pros, I'm gonna prove you wrong! In this section, I'll walk you through the process. I promise, it's not as hard as you think it'll be! And once you do one room, you'll be infected by the wallpapering bug.

All wallpapers are different. I prefer to use temporary versus permanent, given the flexibility it offers for renters as well as people like me who experience sudden and intense urges to change up their space.

If you're unsure what type of wallpaper to choose for your room, I'm here to help. It's true that different rooms call for different wallpaper styles. I'd never put the fun blue stars from my son's nursery in my own bedroom, for example. Here's a guide to wallpapering different rooms that you can take as a loose recommendation. Remember, I always want you to have fun and make your own choices!

OPPOSITE: If you have a room with lots of quirky angles, wallpaper can transform those wonky walls into a magical escape! (Wallpaper by Sara Fitz Studio, sarafitz.com.)

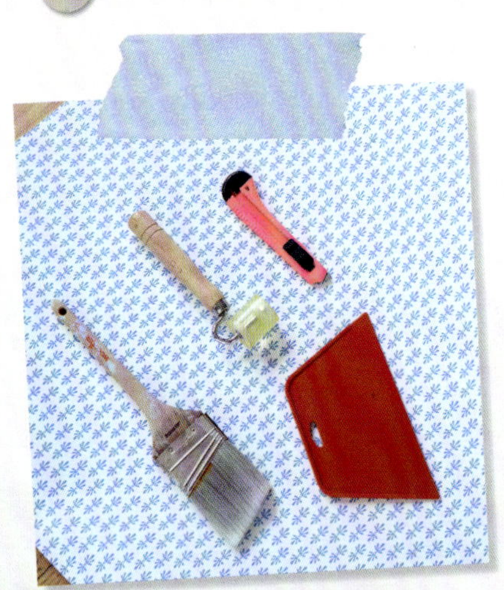

Installing wallpaper in my first-floor bathroom.

LIVING ROOM: It's the heart of your home and should feel like it. You'll want a wallpaper that's more versatile than graphic, since you'll be in here often, and decorating with many different furniture pieces, patterns, and textures. If you're looking for a serene wallpaper that isn't busy, but does feel more interesting than wall paint, consider a colored grass cloth or a muted botanical motif.

BEDROOM: Look for wallpapers that feel peaceful and romantic. Loose florals, tonal chinoiseries, or abstract shapes are a good choice. In the bedroom, I seek muted and relaxing tones. Instead of hot pink, I'd go for a blush. If you are going for more drama, a pattern with contrasting colors, like green and orange or black and white, would certainly be bold. For an added touch of romance, metallic wallpaper feels special and will reflect dim nighttime lighting beautifully. If you're looking to really save, the bedroom is my favorite place for an accent wall. I've often wallpapered just the wall behind a bed—if you don't have a headboard, you could even cut an arched shape out of wallpaper to create the illusion of a headboard!

KITCHEN AND DINING ROOM: I don't wallpaper in a kitchen. Too many messes! In the dining room you're safer, but you still need to beware of food and spillage. Look for vinyl wallpaper for a dining room, which is easy to wipe clean. If your dining room is removed from the rest of the house, it's a great spot for a bold geometric or a colorful, splashy floral!

BATHROOM: Peeling is the last thing you want after putting in the work of installing wallpaper. Bathrooms need moisture-resistant wallpaper due to the constant splashing and humidity that fog it up after a hot shower. I love a subtle nod to the nautical in a bathroom, given the whole water thing. But beware: Nautical decor can get "on the nose" easily. Keep it subtle, doing "coastal" as a blue stripe or a design that loosely references waves.

DEEP SEA FISHING
DROP IN OR CALL CH 4-5420

The How-To

MATERIALS

Wallpapering adhesive and paintbrush
(if your wallpaper isn't prepasted or peel-and-stick)

Smoothing tool

Utility knife

Measuring tape

Straightedge

1. Prepare your wall by spackling and sanding any holes or cracks. Remove outlet covers and light switch panels.
2. Measure the height of your walls and add a few extra inches for trimming at the top and bottom.
3. Roll out your wallpaper. Measure and cut your first panel.
4. If your wallpaper has adhesive, soak the strips in water according to the instructions to activate the glue. If you're using non-pasted wallpaper, apply a thin layer of wallpaper paste to the back of each strip with a brush or roller. If it's peel and stick, peel off about one foot of backing.
5. Position the first strip in the top corner of the wall. Line up the side of the panel with the corner of your wall to ensure it's straight (**A**).
6. To apply the wallpaper, stick the very top on first. Smooth from the top down, using large sweeping strokes with the side of your arm. Focus on two-foot-long sections and work your way down, always checking that the wallpaper lines up with the corner of the wall (**B**). A big smoothing motion with your arm or hand allows the paper less opportunity to grab the wall where it shouldn't. After you're happy with how it's lying, you can smooth out any small bubbles (**C**). If you've got big bubbles to reckon with, I recommend pulling the paper up and starting again rather than fighting the big bubbles, which creates creases and can damage the paper.
7. For the next strip, get up on a stepladder to find where the pattern lines up to the first panel. Align the pattern at the highest point possible, then cut the bottom with scissors, leaving a few inches' excess. You'll have a bit of extra at the top too, which you'll trim afterward as well (**D**).
8. When lining up wallpaper, overlap one piece on top of the other by a tiny amount to make sure there are no gaps.
9. Once all your panels are hung, take a straightedge and cut across the top and bottom (**E**).

A

B

C

D

E

STENCILING

Stencils are awesome. If you don't know how to draw, or lack the steady hand needed for a mural painting, they're perfect for you. But they're also useful for artsy types as well. I don't care how talented a painter you are, there's no way you can create an identical flower fifteen times over on a wall. And why would you want to, when you can use a simple stencil to help you create design perfection?

The first time I stenciled, I bought my template online. I was flipping a Florida bedroom and wanted to create a dramatic yet tonal accent wall. I painted the entire room light blue, then used the stencil to paint a darker blue botanical motif. I was pleasantly surprised by the result: a consistent geometric design that looked almost like real wallpaper!

Once I became addicted to stenciling, I couldn't be stopped. My office wall? Stenciled. My furniture? Stenciled. My freakin' water bottle?! STENCILED! By this point, I had purchased a Cricut machine so that I could cut out my own stencils after drawing a design on my iPad.

But as my ADHD tendencies go, I eventually lost interest in my fancy new machine. When I wanted to impulsively stencil a wall, I realized that I didn't have any acetate paper left that would work with my Cricut. Instead of hopping in the car to buy some, I looked around at what I already had. A shiny corner of packaging in the recycling bin caught my eye. Like a raccoon, I dug for the plastic and pulled it out, holding it up to the light. It shone as brightly as a diamond. THIS COULD WORK!

My foray into *totally* handmade stencils began that day, and it was so easy! I drew a stylized flower on a pad of paper, laid my plastic sheet over it, and traced the flower using a permanent marker. I then cut out my flower with an X-Acto knife, and lo and behold—a stencil! From the trash, nonetheless!

An issue I learned after excitedly stenciling a few flowers onto the wall: I had only one stencil. When you're working with wet paint, it's much more practical to use multiple stencils as you work. That way, when you've completed one stencil and you want it to dry, you can move on to the next spot using a new stencil. If you have three or four, sometimes you're able to keep a consistent rotation going, letting your first stencil dry while you paint a few more—by the time you're done with those, your first stencil will be dry enough to pick up and start the process again.

So, when I make my own stencils, I always make a few, ensuring they come out relatively consistent across the board.

My enthusiasm for stencils has taken me far and wide, from the initial Florida bedroom to my old office in Yonkers, to my Connecticut home, and eventually into the arms of Drew Barrymore herself. Yep, I was filming segments as a guest design commentator on her show, and she asked me during a commercial break if I'd return and film a stenciling tutorial for her viewers. You read that right—Drew, HERSELF, said she'd seen my videos and personally invited me back on the show. Turns out, Drew had been bit by the stencil bug, too! It's unavoidable, people. And she was serious about her invitation! I got an email a few weeks later and got to perform a stenciling demo to a live audience—and an audience of national television viewers!

For this next tutorial, try it over kitchen or bathroom tile you dislike. It'll be quite the transformation! Stenciling always goes quicker with a friend, and it's much easier that way—but like all projects I share, if I can do it myself, so can you!

The How-To

Here, I'll show you how I stenciled my bathroom floor tiles. If you plan on stenciling a wall, you can refer to these instructions as well, but use regular wall paint!

MATERIALS

STENCIL:

Plastic sheet or acetate paper

A design you've drawn, traced, or printed out

Sharpie

Utility knife

PAINTING:

Tile paint:
I used Stix

Various colors of chalk paint

Polyurethane glossy topcoat

Adhesive spray or double-sided tape
(In this tutorial, I used painter's tape, but have found the two options I listed to be much better at the job, with quantifiably less mess)

Stenciling brushes
(though a foam brush or normal paintbrushes will do)

Paint roller

1 To make your stencil:

- **a.** Place acetate paper over your design. It's very easy to put the plastic over your computer screen if you're tracing something digital! You'll need to measure the dimensions of the tile you're covering to ensure your stencil is the same size as the tile square.
- **b.** Make a few duplicates.
- **c.** Cut out your designs with scissors or an X-Acto knife.

2 To decide which colors you'll use with your stencil, paint a trial by using your stencil on a big piece of paper. Play around with your stencil size and your colors until you're totally satisfied with the final design.

3 The first step in painting any floor is to thoroughly clean it.

4 Prep for painting your floor by taping around the walls, base of your sink, tub, and toilet.

5 After your floor is debris- and dust-free, begin rolling your first coat of tile paint directly over the existing tile (**A**). Make sure not to paint yourself into a corner. I do this literally every time I've painted a floor.

6 Let the first coat dry completely, then follow with a second coat (**B**, **C**). After that's dry, determine whether the paint is opaque enough. If not, grab a glass of wine and go in for coat number three!

CONTINUED

A
B
C

D
E
F
G

7. By now, you're probably in bed. Good! Wait until tomorrow to regain your sanity and strength, and to make sure your floor is totally dry.
8. Now for the fun! Start in the far corner of your bathroom. Place your first stencil down over a tile, securing it in place with your spray adhesive or double-sided tape (**D**).
9. Begin filling in your stencil (**E**). Start with a little bit of paint and see how far it gets you. The less paint you use, the less likely it is that your design will bleed. And listen carefully: You're not *painting*. You're *dabbing*. Instead of filling your stencil in with brushstroke motions, dab lightly at the design. When dabbing, you can color outside the lines, and you'll end up with a clean design. Be warned that if you use a brushing motion, it's likely that tiny paintbrush bristles will sneak into crevices they don't belong in, bringing paint with them. We don't want this. Your design is NOT going to come out perfect—get your head around that before you proceed—but we're doing everything we can to make it look as near-perfect as possible.
10. Let that stencil dry while you tape up and paint the next few. Once your first motif has dried, lift up the stencil (**F**, **G**) and smile proudly at the resulting design.
11. Continue stenciling until the floor is complete. Pro tip: In hard-to-reach areas such as around the toilet, save those tiles for last. You can cut your stencils, if you make enough, to get a perfect fit in awkward corners. I save the corners for last so that I don't cut into my stencils until the whole floor (or wall!) is done.
12. After your stencil designs dry and you've fixed any mistakes with a small paintbrush, you're ready to seal it all in.
13. With your paint roller, cover the floor evenly with your poly topcoat. You can use a brush or a roller for this. A brush is great for corners, while a large roller ensures a smooth finish. For good measure, and especially in a high-traffic bathroom, paint two to three coats.
14. Look at that transformed floor!

NOTE: See Appendix for a selection of stencil templates I made for you!

CHAPTER 2

DO IT YOURSELF

Why do I cringe slightly at the acronym "DIY"? It's what I do for a living, for God's sake, yet the term feels so supercharged with associations that I've come to be wary of it. It could be the grammatical inaccuracy that tends to follow the term. "I DIYed my own chicken coop!!" Okay . . . so you "do it yourself-ed" your own chicken coop? I can't get over it. Some people refer to me as a "DIYer." I read it back to myself, shuddering. I'm a "Do it *yourselfer*?"

Don't get me wrong, I love being a DIYer, making things on my own. But not everything. I focus on projects that would be way too expensive if I *didn't* DIY them. So yes, I make my own lampshades. But I use designer fabric and add custom trim—you could pay a seamstress to make one for you, and it'd cost hundreds of dollars. Instead of teaching you how to make an air-dry phone case (you can head to my TikTok for that tutorial), I'm reserving the DIY projects in this book for approaches that will save you *real* money. These are projects that you'd normally hire a pro for. Instead, I'll show you how to do the real thing, which will save you hundreds, if not thousands, of dollars. And 90 percent of the projects don't involve power tools.

I began DIYing my home out of desperation. I *wanted* to create a thoughtful, luxurious interior, but I was hindered by high prices and not having any idea where to start even if I could've afforded to have something custom made. So instead of researching professionals in my area, I spent time learning how to do things on my own. Back in our grandparents' day, everything was DIY—especially if you were lower- to middle-class. Mothers made clothing for their families, stenciled their walls to add interest to their dining rooms, and knew how to patch up their old furniture. I'm not saying we should go back in time, and I'm grateful that women no longer have to stay home to sew. But people knew how to do so much more for themselves than they do now. And don't get me wrong, I *AM* lazy. I am constantly ordering dinner from Uber Eats, or Instacart-ing my groceries to the front door. It's fun to online-shop for home decor!

Creating a shadowbox with vintage matchbooks. DIY what you enjoy and learn the skills to create items you love.

I'm not asking you to sacrifice any modern amenities—I certainly won't be. But I do know that there's a sense of pride involved with learning skills and creating tangible items with your own two hands. It's a particularly strong strain of self pride that I experience only after creating something new for my home or for my family. When I learned how to correctly anchor a screw into the wall, I felt like I could do ANYTHING.

So, DIY is not only good for your wallet, it's also good for your brain. Creating beauty from scratch is a skill we've lost over the years, and I think we should try to bring it back. We don't need to revert to homesteading, or quit our day jobs, but trying a weekend project every now and again can't hurt in your quest for self-development. It's a wonderful feeling, to be proud of yourself.

So I hope you've picked up the tools I told you to buy. Maybe your first "DIY" could be decorating your new toolbox or tool bag. Flower stickers, paint, wallpaper scraps, Mod Podge—you name it! And after you're done, get ready to totally transform your home without breaking the bank.

A note about these projects: For each DIY, there are a few materials that you'll likely need but I'm guessing you already have, like scissors, pencils, and measuring tape. For the sake of reducing redundancy, I've omitted these basic household materials from your shopping lists, but if you're running low, make sure to restock before you get started!

HANGING A GALLERY WALL

Have you ever stared at a big, blank, white wall and thought, "How on earth am I going to decorate this?!" Well, if you looked up from your book and stared aghast at the empty wall in front of you, know that I'm not a psychic. I don't actually know that you have empty walls. But I do know that you're looking for decor advice from me, and I also know how intimidating it can be to decorate an expansively blank wall. Trust me, I've been there. I was so overwhelmed by my living room wall's vastness that I spent a whole year pretending it didn't exist.

Every wall is different. Some are tall. Some are small. Some are short. Some are long. Some are adorned with beadboard, while others lack even the simplest crown molding at the top. And given the wide variety of wall types in your home, it's important to understand that each deserves its own special treatment when it comes to hanging art. This technique works best on a larger wall.

I FINALLY ADDRESSED the overwhelmingly large wall in my own house after I'd taken a Saturday afternoon to sort through all of the art I'd been storing in my basement. I was inspired to tackle my problem wall because I'd recently hung a gallery wall for my mom and dad, who were facing that same "big wall phobia." To tackle their wall, I created an easy system for hanging multiple pieces of art in a neat and curated way.

Selecting Your Pieces

I decided that a vintage seafarer look would work for my wall, and I pulled out all the sailing art from my collection. When it comes to a gallery wall, I've created my own rule: The paintings must relate to one another in *one* specific way. For example, my selections are related to each other through their nautical theme. But there were a few outliers I wanted to include, like the sign I'd bought at my favorite antiques store's closing sale, which fit in with the rest of my nautical art because the letters were blue.

So, say you wanted to hang a gallery wall to display your cat art, but needed to fill in a few gaps since you're short on sixteenth-century feline portraits. Take a look at the colors in your spread. Maybe you see lots of yellow. You could then fill in your gap with a painting of a sunflower to complement the calico cat to its left. Or maybe your cats are all in gold frames—you could throw in a seventies concert poster that also has a gold frame. But don't feel that these are strict rules. The best gallery walls are extremely eclectic! I love a gallery wall filled with different-color frames. The idea is that you wouldn't frame *one* piece in black while the other five pieces are in white frames. You're looking for visual cohesion, even if you have only one unifying feature that marries your pieces into one greater look.

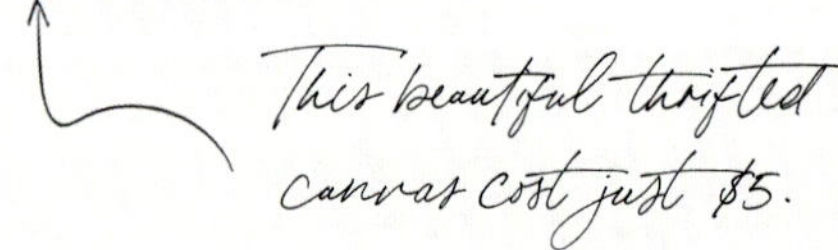

This beautiful thrifted canvas cost just $5.

MORE
UPSTAIRS
William Wegman
Hello
Nature

The How-To

MATERIALS

Scrap paper or cardboard

Measuring tape

Painter's tape

Hammer

Picture hangers

1 Find some cardboard, large scrap paper, or even newsprint. Lay your art down over the paper and trace the shape of it with a pen (**A**).

2 Cut out your shape, which is now a perfect representation of the size of the art you'll be hanging (**B**).

3 Now, we need to find out where the nail goes. To find the right point on your paper, we have to look at the back of our art. For a wire-hung painting, measure the width of your artwork to find the center (**C**). Then measure the height of your nail: from the top center of the painting to the top of the wire (when stretched). For a bracket-hung painting, take the same measurements from top to bottom and side to side to find the exact location where your bracket will be hung.

4 Transfer those measurements of width and height directly onto the paper with an X (**D**). Or a heart. Or a dot. I don't care, just make sure you can see it!

CONTINUED

Clare Rule

Take a look at the consistent spacing of my pieces. This is a "Clare Rule": You want the same-size "channel" running through all your pieces. So if you're hanging a painting 3 inches away from another, make sure that there's a 3-inch gap between *all* paintings. Three inches from the bottom of one painting to the bottom of another painting, and 3 inches from the left edge of one painting to the right edge of its neighbor. I think of it as a margin that needs to be consistent. This approach creates an intentional look that unifies varying pieces, instead of looking like a haphazard assortment of randomly spaced frames. And again, my rules are loose: If you have an intention to your approach, I believe in it! Creative whims should always be followed, especially if you're experiencing that all-too-familiar tingling urge to do something crazy that won't be quieted unless you *try it*. Caulk exists for a reason, and nails can always be removed.

A

B

C

D

E

F

G

H

5. Place the paper on your wall with tape (**E**). You can play around with your paper templates on the floor before you tape them up, or just move them around the wall until you're happy!

6. Grab your hammer and the trimmed-out piece of paper (put your art to the side for the time being). Nail directly into the scrap paper on the X you've marked (**F**). I love this approach, because you're bound to feel less nervous about putting a big nail in the wall when you know that if you swing and miss, the hammer will ding your cardboard, not your wall.

7. Pull off your scrap paper to reveal a perfectly placed nail (**G**)!

8. Hang your painting on the nail, step back, and smile smugly to yourself (**H**). You're now a professional gallery wall hanger, and you simply can't be stopped!

Cardboard templates helped me create perfect spacing between a diverse array of art that could otherwise appear mismatched and random.

TRANSFORMING A LUXURIOUS PRIMARY SUITE

At my core, I am a bedroom dweller. In fact, I'm currently writing this section from my bed! I finagled a way to move my desk next to the bed, and close enough that I can reach the computer. Turns out, a mouse works pretty well when you're moving it around on a fitted sheet. I've got a shih tzu to my right, and my baby is to my left, grabbing my fingers as they try to type. The perfect work-from-home setup!

Something about the bedroom just feels so safe to me. I prefer to work in a closed-off space, and of course I like being comfortable. So, each night when I edit my content, I do it from bed. I spent a few months in my new bedroom just "making it work" with minimal decor and sad beige walls. I was renovating most of the downstairs by hand, so I didn't have time or energy to put into my bedroom. Plus I was pregnant, with little energy to even get out of bed some days.

But during my many hours spent in bed, staring up at the ceiling while battling nausea, heartburn, and my son's foot, which was sweetly wedged into my upper ribs, I started to devise a plan that would turn my bedroom from drab to fab. In the next section, I'll walk you through the major upgrades I implemented to make my bedroom feel like my very own safe, pretty little haven.

LEFT: My bedroom a few months into living in our new house: lackluster, uninspiring, and stagnant.

OPPOSITE: A fresh coat of paint, some designer fabric, and a bit of creative thinking was all I needed to upgrade my room.

After

Creating a No-Sew, Custom Bed Canopy

To me, the most luxurious bedrooms all have something in common: a canopy bed. From the bedrooms of Mario Buatta (my favorite interior designer!) to Marie Antoinette, canopy beds are a staple in elegant homes and have been for centuries.

When I was in grad school, I used to walk to the Met with my sketchbook to study the period rooms. I'd spend hours sketching the historic drapery of the past and yearning for my own bed canopy in the process. Like most custom upholstery, bed canopies are extremely expensive. You could expect to pay anywhere from $2,000 to $20,000 for a bespoke canopy, which renders them inaccessible for those of us lacking in "the big bucks."

My idea to DIY a canopy came to me while shopping for curtain rods at Lowe's. It occurred to me that if I installed rods on my walls and ceiling, they'd do a great job of holding up fabric—pretty obvious, but it felt like I'd been struck with a near-revolutionary revelation.

My bed, being king-size, is pretty large and needed two rolls of fabric to account for the width of the bed. I also needed plenty of yardage to span the height of the wall and slanted ceiling. To hang the canopy, all you need is curtain rods. I found mine on Amazon. I hung the lower one to hold the fabric against the wall. The upper one was a bit more involved, since I had to get ceiling curtain rod hooks from the hardware store, which would suspend the top rod from the ceiling. Once those rods were mounted, I climbed up on the bed and got to hanging! Now our bedroom feels like a palatial suite. Every single night, I get happy when I look at it.

It took me only an afternoon to "construct," and though my canopy isn't exactly a seventeenth-century four-poster extravaganza, it adds a significant layer of comfort and pattern to my bedroom.

A NOTE ON BUYING YOUR FABRIC: Because designer fabric is pricey, I am a frequent shopper of warehouses and fabric discount stores. These often-hidden gems sell fabric by the roll, and though you may have to sort through rolls of dated nineties floral and sports-themed motifs, if you keep an open mind, you may just strike gold. I found my fabric at a major discount and loved the green color that matched my walls perfectly (note: Always take paint samples with you when fabric shopping!). Make sure to measure your walls, ceiling, and bed before you go searching for the perfect fabric, so you can purchase the correct amount on the spot. Nothing worse than getting home and realizing you're two yards short!

My design sketch for the canopy I'd envisioned.

The How-To

MATERIALS

Two heavy-duty curtain rods

Two sturdy "O" ceiling-mount brackets (these won't come with your curtain rods!)

Screws and anchors (your curtain rods probably include these in their packages)

Drill

HeatnBond hem tape

Fabric

1. Roll out your fabric (**A**). You'll likely have to connect two lengths of fabric to account for the width of your bed, so keep that in mind.

2. Measure your fabric length and add about six or more extra inches at the top for the curtain rod pocket (**B**). If you're using two pieces of fabric, make sure that you match the pattern up so that the two panels look cohesive—this means that one piece may be longer than the other. That's fine. Don't worry about trimming it until later on.

3. Very carefully cut your beautiful fabric to the length desired (**C**).

4. To connect two lengths of fabric together into one extra-wide panel, you'll be ironing them together using hemming tape. For a clean "hem" line, fold back the cut edge of your first panel to hide it. Use fabric tape to "hem" the fold (**D**). Now run your tape lengthwise down the edge of your second panel, where it'll connect to the top panel.

5. Put your "hemmed" first panel over the second panel, and iron your pieces together.

CONTINUED

I BOUGHT THIS HEMMING TAPE at Michaels, and it is a lifesaver for those of us who have been procrastinating taking those sewing lessons. To use, simply lay your tape down on fabric. If you're "hemming," fold your fabric back over the tape. If you're connecting two pieces, simply lay the top piece over the taped bottom piece. To keep a straight line, use pins. Heat up your iron and run it over the fabric to activate your tape.

A

B

C

D

Clare Rule

Remember to think carefully about your measurements: Would you like the canopy to reach the floor? Do you want a gathered or a straight look? Be thoughtful and careful here. Repeat to yourself: "Measure twice, cut once."

E

F

G

H

Time to hang!

6. To determine the size of the rod pocket, measure your curtain rod's circumference. Make the pocket by folding the top of the panel down. The folded fabric should be as thick as the circumference of your rod, plus about an inch to allow for wiggle room. To create your pocket, place tape along the inside of your fold and iron over the fabric slowly to activate your tape. Now that you've created a pocket at the top of your panel, slide it onto the rod to hang (**E**).
7. "Hem" the bottom of your fabric by folding it over, taping, and ironing (**F**).
8. Dig your drill out of the tool bag (**G**), and head to the bedroom! You're going to hang the first rod on the wall above the bed.
9. Mount your curtain brackets to the wall, using anchors or drilling into studs (**H**).

CONTINUED

FACTORS TO CONSIDER when mounting your curtain rod: The lower the rod, the closer the fabric will hang above your head. Do you want sconces on either side of the canopy? Choose the height of your rod wisely.

10 To determine where to hang your ceiling brackets (the "O" brackets [I]), use a straightedge to draw two vertical lines from the bottom wall brackets up to the ceiling. Make two pencil lines perpendicular to your headboard at these widths to indicate the width of your rod.

11 Decide how far out over the bed you'd like your canopy to hang. Say you've chosen to mount the rod 3 feet out over the bed. Measure 3 feet out over the bed, using the width markers you made in step 10 to keep the top brackets in line with the bottom ones. Mark your screw holes with a pencil.

12 Place your "O" brackets on your marks and drill them in (J)! Remember, these need to be very sturdy, and if you're not drilling directly into a wood beam like I did, use anchors!

13 Hang your bottom curtain rod up on the brackets (K).

CONTINUED

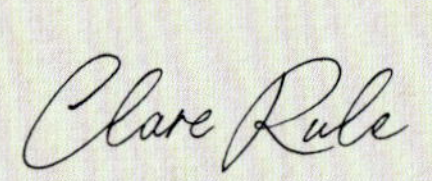

After you've hung the canopy, take a few extra steps to perfect it—smooth the fabric with a garment steamer and cinch your fabric to get a perfectly gathered look by pulling and compressing the pocket fabric.

THE ANGLE OF the canopy draping is up to you. The farther out you take the ceiling rod over the bed, the steeper the slant (and in my opinion, the cozier the canopy).

I

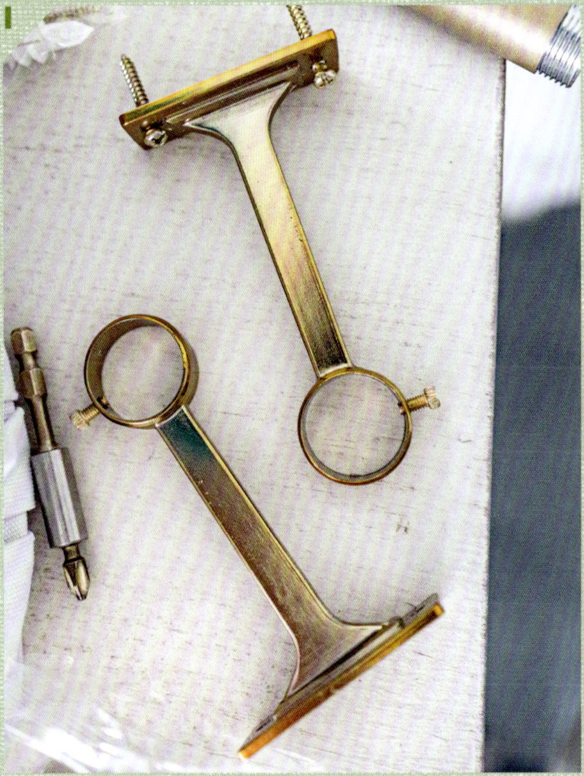

J

K

L
M
N
O

14 Insert the ceiling rod into your fabric pocket, bunching or neatening it as you'd like (**L**).

15 Hang up your ceiling rod, fabric attached (**M**)!

16 Now pull the bottom of your panel over and behind your wall rod (**N**). Leave excess fabric above the rod if you'd like a more relaxed, curving drape, or pull it tight for an angular look (**O**).

No-Sew, Custom-Look Fabric Lampshades

Sewing is one DIY technique I haven't learned, and though I know I probably should . . . I've found an alternative to sewing that works just fine, in my opinion. And this way, I can share tips with those of you who also fear needles (not the kind in the doctor's office—the sewing ones that are always IMPOSSIBLE to get thread through!) For this project, I'll show you how I created lampshades using the remnants of the fabric from my canopy. Using the same fabric on my shades created a very high-end, custom look in my bedroom. Plus, I'll also show you how gold spray paint can elevate the inside of a lampshade, adding a beautiful reflective glow.

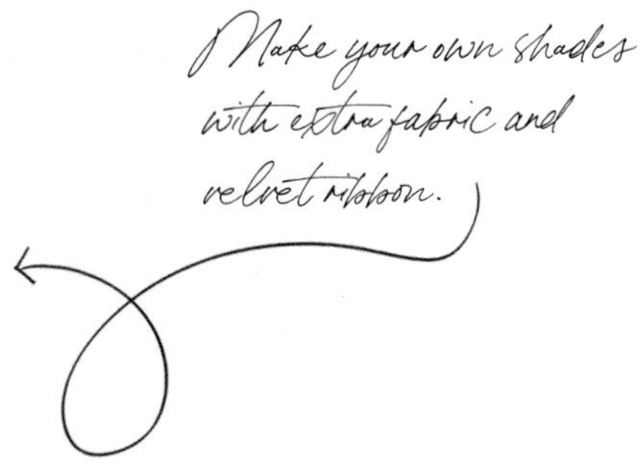

The How-To

MATERIALS

HeatnBond hem tape

Gold spray paint

Fabric

Decorative ribbon

Lampshade

1 Head outside with a drop cloth and a mask. Spray the inside of your lampshade with a gold spray paint (**A**). You might need two coats. Avoid overspraying, as this will cause the paint to drip and create unsightly patterns!

2 Lay your fabric flat and mark how much length you need to cover the circumference of the shade (**B**). Give yourself a few extra inches to work with in case of any mishaps! Then measure the height of your shade, adding 3 inches for the hem. My shade was 10 inches high, so I gave myself 13 inches width on my fabric.

3 Cut out your rectangle, making sure that it fits all the way around your shade (**C**).

4 Flip your freshly cut strip of fabric design-side down and place your shade at one end, centered. Mark the edge of the shade at top and bottom (**D**). This is where you'll fold the fabric over to create a "hem."

CONTINUED

I RECOMMEND USING a drum shade for this project. Slanted empire shades are hard to wrap in a straight line! And make sure you're using an unpleated shade so that the fabric wraps smoothly.

Hem tape is a great way to make custom pieces without knowing how to sew.

A
B
Clare Rule
Measure twice, cut once!
C
D

E

F

G

H

I

5. Remove the shade and fold your fabric (**E**). Pin down the fabric to keep your fold in place, and start putting hem tape underneath the fold, all the way to the end.
6. Iron over your fold to "hem" (**F**).
7. Add hem tape directly onto the top and bottom edges of the shade to adhere the fabric to it (**G**, **H**). Iron the fabric to the shade.
8. Cut decorative ribbon and attach to the top and bottom of the shade with your hem tape (**I**). Iron to secure!

High-end designers oftentimes swath their clients' bedrooms with one gorgeous fabric across the board.

AN ORDERLY AND WELCOMING ENTRY

Your entryway is where you introduce yourself to the world. When you walk into your home, you should feel embraced by your own personal style. Plus, the entryway is how your home makes its first (and last) impression to your guests. The challenge, though, in embracing personal style in an entryway is that you can't forget about function. It's where you put on your coat and boots, where you hang your dog leashes, and where you haul in big packages. For practical purposes, your entryway must be clear of clutter and easy to move through, and it should be an organizational workforce.

Not only was my entryway organizationally challenged, it lacked any aesthetic charm. If you're battling a similar entryway conundrum, read on to get inspired by my own project.

The entryway, in all its dated glory, when we moved into the house.

After

Easy Wall Paneling

There are plenty of ways to transform a plain wall, from changing up the paint color to applying wallpaper. If you're looking to add more architectural interest in your home, wall paneling can be a great approach. Most modern homes are devoid of wall detail, which is more common in prewar buildings. But I think paneling can really warm up a space, and you can personalize it to your liking. Don't be intimidated by sawing and using a nail gun; it's very simple to install your own paneling if you know what to buy and how to do it. I loved the way paneling transformed my entryway, and think it's a no-brainer project, especially for small spaces.

ABOVE: My sketch for a fresh and modern entryway.

SPRINGS
Springs

The How-To

MATERIALS

¾" × 3½" × 8' PVC trim

Box saw

Nail gun with ½" brad nails

Caulk

Caulk gun

Rubber gloves

SOME HARDWARE STORES actually will cut trim to size for you! Make sure you bring exact measurements to give to an employee. If you're lucky enough to have a local store that offers cutting, you get to skip the step of sawing it on your own.

1. Measure your wall (**A**). Decide how many "panels" you want. I chose to have eight, each about one foot apart.

2. Mark where you'll nail the PVC trim to the wall by measuring across (**B**). Each trim piece should be spaced equally. Make one mark at the bottom, and one mark at the top of the wall, ensuring your trim will be perfectly straight when hung.

3. Take your sketch to your local hardware store, where you'll buy your trim. Purchase as many pieces of ¾ inch by 3½ inch trim as you need. I bought mine from Home Depot, and they were 8 feet long (**C**). If you're trimming out a corner, like me, you can buy two half-width pieces to put adjunctly in the corner.

4. Hopefully you've read the list of materials needed for this project first, and picked up a box saw along with your trim and other tools. Here's the cool part: You're going to saw your own pieces! Mark off the length you need each piece to be (**D**).

CONTINUED

A
B
C
D
HOLY CROSS

E

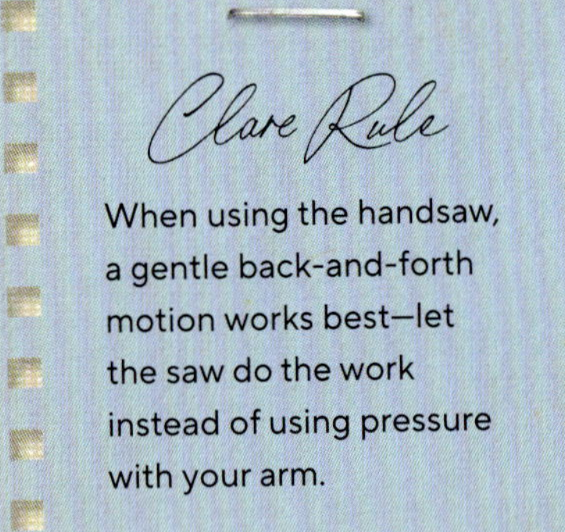

Clare Rule

When using the handsaw, a gentle back-and-forth motion works best—let the saw do the work instead of using pressure with your arm.

F

G

5 Insert the trim into your box saw base, lining up your mark with the two slats in the middle, which are designed to create a right angle. Put your saw through the slats and, with a sleight of hand, run the saw back and forth over your wood (**E**).

6 Mark the center-width point of the top and bottom of each piece (**F**). Do this on the side of the trim that will show—it helps you center the piece vertically on the wall where you're hanging it.

7 Put your first piece up on the wall, matching the midpoints on your trim to the marks you previously drew onto the floor and ceiling. Your trim should be perfectly vertical, sitting in the center of the top and bottom points you marked previously.

8 Use a nail gun or a hammer to install brad nails (**G**). I started with a nail at the top and a nail at the bottom to make sure it ran straight, then put two nails in the middle.

CONTINUED

9. If you're installing corner pieces, follow the same process as above, making sure that your two pieces are close together without a gap.

10. Caulk the sides of your trim to ensure no gaps can be seen (**H**). This creates a polished and professional look. Wearing rubber gloves, run your fingers down the sides to smooth out the caulk (**I**).

11. Caulk over the nails (**J**). Once dry, sand the caulk so you have a smooth surface for painting!

12. Wipe down your surface and begin painting (**K**). (See page 62 for painting tips.)

H
I
J
K

Click-in "Slate" Flooring

While I've always appreciated the warmth and character of natural wood and love the way it looks in most of my house, my entryway floor had seen better days. Years of wear had left behind deep scratches, discoloration, and warping in some areas. Plus, the previous owners had installed a faux-Mediterranean-style mosaic at the front door. Needless to say, I wanted that mosaic gone—or at least covered up.

Restoring the flooring would've been a time-consuming, labor-intensive job with no guarantee of perfection—but I hadn't considered other options until I saw a vinyl click-in flooring system at Home Depot. Vinyl, ew. But wait, the tiles *seriously* looked like real stone. And slate, no less! I really love a slate or brick floor in the mudroom but could definitely not afford to have real slate installed. So I decided to try out the vinyl!

Once I opened the box, I saw that the faux slate I'd selected looked surprisingly realistic. It captures the elegance of a natural slate floor but is more resistant to scratches, scuffs, and water damage. This was a game changer for me. Wood floors are beautiful, but they can be unforgiving; the entryway floor had been badly beaten up by my family in less than one year of living

Before

The mosaic tile I couldn't live with.

here, between stroller wheels leaving black marks, my shih tzus' scratches, and my own mishaps (I'd scratched the floor with tools, accidentally spilled deck stain in the far corner, and overall it just was screaming for help).

The vinyl tiles, on the other hand, are forgiving and durable, standing up to the everyday chaos of life in the Sullivan household. Plus, because they were an inexpensive "reno" option, I'm not so stressed about scratches, spills, and overall wear and tear. The waterproof nature of the vinyl is great for when we inevitably track in mud from the garden, or snow after an afternoon of shoveling.

But most of all, I just like the look, and *love* pretending my mudroom opens up to an English country cottage garden. The "slate" floor just feels like it would belong there!

The How-To

MATERIALS

Click-in vinyl flooring tiles

Pencil or chalk

T square or straightedge

Rubber mallet

China marker

Utility knife

Jigsaw with fine-tooth blades (for easier cuts), **and if you use a jigsaw:**

Clamps

Wood blocks

Templating tool (optional)

1 Deep-clean your floor to ensure you're installing on top of a grime-free surface. We don't want to lock in any dirt or dust bunnies!

2 Plan your layout. I wanted the tiles to stagger. I planned the first row by starting against the wall, and then worked out my pattern for the second row based off the first row. Lay out a few tiles in a line on the floor before clicking them together to see how they look before you make any cuts or snap them together.

3 To begin your installation, start in a corner and lay down a tile, making sure that it's lying in the correct direction to snap the second tile into its groove (**A**). Once you've matched the grooves of your first two tiles, they should snap together when you apply pressure from above. For me, I knew the fit was right if the snap came easily. I used a hammer only when I got to the end and had to work in some tight areas.

4 Here's where we get a little technical: When you encounter a corner, or some irregular door trim, you'll have to cut a tile to give it a perfect fit (**B**). To mark your tile to cut, you could create a template from paper, or go the easy route: Use a templating tool to re-create the shape of the corner (**C**, **D**), then trace that shape onto your tile using a china marker.

5 If you're planning on using a jigsaw, which makes the job faster, make sure you are fully aware of all safety precautions in the instructions. Tie your hair back, use protective gear, and clamp EVERYTHING down. You don't want pieces flying around. And you really don't want to get your hair or fingers caught. Read the instructions in your manual, and don't count on me to guarantee your safety! If you're confident in your jigsaw skills after trying a few test runs, let's get into it:

a. Use a fine-tooth blade that works on plastic and vinyl.

b. Secure the tile to your table, with the cut line hanging off the edge, using wood blocks and clamps (**E**).

c. Create a straightedge for cutting your line with a large piece of wood clamped over the table and tile. Adjust your tile so that when your saw is against the straightedge, the blade is directly on your cutting line.

d. Begin sawing from one end, SLOWLY tracing the line with your blade (**F**).

CONTINUED

A
B
RYOBI
C
D
E
F

G

H

I

A long board secured to my kitchen island with clamps creates a straightedge that the jigsaw can push against as a guide for a perfect straight line.

6 If you chose to forgo the saw, I hold no judgment. It took me years to get comfortable with a saw! As a solution, you're going to use a straightedge to cut the line you drew on the tile.

a. Make multiple scoring lines with your knife until you reach more than halfway through the thickness of the tile with your cut (**G**).

b. Place the tile over a table edge, hold down one side, and push down on the side hanging over the edge (**H**). If you've made enough cuts, the tile will break off cleanly! If not, keep on cuttin'.

7 Install the rest of your tiles (**I**). Keep in mind that you can't go back to fix loose tiles without tearing up the entire floor, so make sure you are positive each tile is fully locked into its neighbor before continuing.

8 Do a final sweep of any dirt and debris, and admire your new flooring.

No-Sew Upholstered Bench Cushion

I chose to DIY upholster the bench cushion in my entry because, let's face it, custom furniture prices are no joke. Instead of spending a small fortune on a custom piece, I decided to try upholstering for the first time ever! I found a roll of amazing vintage designer fabric at my favorite fire-sale store, Marden's. It was just $10 a roll! To find designer fabric at a discount, check thrift stores, fabric remnant outlets, and clearance bins at stores. I had plenty of extra yardage to ensure that I wouldn't be super nervous to take on this project as a beginner. If I messed up on the first try, I knew I had extra fabric for a second try. I love the way this cushion came out and would encourage you to try my steps on any sort of surface—a chair, bench, stool, or ottoman. Turns out that a staple gun, some surplus foam, scrap wood, and clearance fabric can create total beauty!

BEFORE I BEGIN this tutorial, I need to get something off my chest—I cheated. Well, sort of. I had an extra piece of plywood, but it wasn't the right size. I had my contractor friend (thanks, T. K.!) cut it down for me. But if you don't have a contractor on the premises, purchase your wood at Home Depot or another store that offers cutting services. They'll chop it to the right size for you!

After

The How-To

MATERIALS

Fabric yardage

Staple gun

Plywood

Large sheet of foam (3"+ width)

X-Acto knife

1. With your board cut to the right size, lay it down over your piece of foam. Trace the outline of the wood directly onto the foam (**A**).
2. With an X-Acto knife, cut along your line. You will need to make multiple cuts to get through the foam!
3. Lay your fabric over the foam to determine how much you'll need to use (**B**). Ensure there's enough to cover the edges, plus a few added inches where you'll secure the fabric underneath.
4. Cut your fabric (**C**).
5. Put your foam on top of the plywood and start folding the corners of the fabric (**D**). I used pins to secure each corner in place while I created pleats. Make sure that the pattern is centered and lying straight! To create a pleated look in your corner, smooth the fabric along the corner. With one finger holding down the fabric on the corner, create a pleat on the left by folding the excess fabric and bringing it to the corner. Repeat on the right, securing both folded sides at the bottom of your corner. Pin your pleat in place temporarily and repeat this process on your next three corners.
6. Pull your fabric tight and neat, ensuring you have no wrinkles. Flip your cushion over and, with your staple gun, begin attaching the excess fabric on the bottom to your plywood (**E**). Make sure that your corners are pulled tight to maintain their nice crease.
7. Trim excess fabric from the bottom (**F**), and flip over your brand-new, beautiful custom bench cushion!

A
B
C
D
E
F

BATHROOMS

Bathrooms are, in my opinion, the most misunderstood rooms in a house. For some strange reason, landlords and homeowners alike seem to share a belief that they should be stark, basic rooms with no color, save for a taupe tile or gray countertop. I'd hypothesize that this is because everyone's going for a *clean* look in the bathroom—it's the place you go to *get* clean, after all. But why can't bathrooms be more *fun*?! I get it, resale value is important. You don't want to install pink tile if you're unsure how it'll perform once you're ready to jump coop and sell house. But what about injecting color into the walls with a temporary wallpaper? Or hanging some colorful art? I think small spaces, like bathrooms, are the best places for making a splash.

Tile Paint

Best budget alternative to dated bathroom tile? Paint! This is a project I've been yearning to take on. I've seen many viral videos of people painting their bathroom tiles. Though it seems ridiculous at first, I can totally get behind the idea after learning about the miracle of tile paint. My new (older) house has very dated bathrooms that I decided would provide the perfect canvas for this approach. In all honesty, buying my first house rendered me pretty broke, and this idea serves as a smart temporary fix for a few years while I save up for more costly, permanent improvements.

My bathroom when we moved in: dated lights and all white.

After
LE SAVON

The How-To

MATERIALS

Chalk paint

Polyurethane glossy topcoat

Small paint roller

Paintbrush

Painter's tape

1. Prep your tiles by taping around the outside of the pieces you want to paint (**A**). Be careful to tape over grout as well, to ensure your paint doesn't bleed through.
2. Paint your first coat of chalk paint with the paintbrush in a thin, even coat (**B**).
3. After letting the paint dry for a couple of hours, go in with another coat of chalk paint (**C**).
4. Let that dry, then prepare for your final coat of gloss by pouring the polyurethane into a tray (**D**).
5. With your small paint roller covered in the gloss, lightly roll it over your painted tiles (**E**).
6. After waiting for it to completely dry, remove your tape to reveal your freshly redone tiles (**F**)!

A
B
C
D
E
F

PAINTING KITCHEN CABINETS

The first room I wanted to redo in my new house was the kitchen. It was a decent enough floor plan, with a two-seater island and an L-shape run of wall cabinets. The issue was the cabinets themselves. They were redone thirty-some years ago. The cabinets were a warm (let's put it frankly—orange) lacquered, cheap remnant of the nineties. But having just closed on the house, forking over a down payment and closing costs, as well as our first mortgage bill, there was NO way I was about to pay for a construction team, new appliances, custom cabinets, and marble countertops.

Sometimes you're forced to work with what you have. The exciting thing about moving to the suburbs was that I didn't have a landlord to answer to. I am she; she is me. Being my own landlord means that I'm free to make any and all DIY changes, for better *or* worse. I was a little nervous about how I could make my kitchen prettier without messing it up completely, but I shrugged off the worry, assuring myself—"I've done this before."

And I *had*! It's not my first rodeo when it comes to kitchen cabinet painting. I know it all

too well—and it's a dreary, exasperating, and exhausting task. It takes DAYS to do it right. In prior projects, I painted cabinets the old-fashioned way, sanding the wood, painting on a primer, waiting a day for that to dry, and then continuing with multiple coats of paint. The drying time was the most excruciating aspect of the project. And after the color went on, I still hadn't finished—they needed a topcoat, too. I wondered if there was a better way to tackle the project.

So I was over the moon—but a little skeptical—when I found out about a product that does all of this for you. I'm sure there are a couple of brands, but the one I went with was called Beyond Paint. Apparently this formula works as a primer, base, and topcoat all in one. They even claim that you don't need to bother with sanding.

I was thrilled to find out that the product actually works, cutting your project time down by about two whole days. It looked nice, too! My black countertops, which I absolutely hated, suddenly looked clean and modern against white cabinets. Once again, I'm here to show you that you don't need a construction team to make adjustments to your home that will both beautify and modernize it.

The How-To

MATERIALS

Painter's tape

Paintbrushes

Screwdriver

Paint roller

Paint tray

Drop cloths

All-purpose furniture paint

1. Clean all of your surfaces *thoroughly* (**A**).
2. Remove all doors and drawer fronts, using a screwdriver to remove the brackets (**B**, **C**).
3. With your screwdriver, remove all hardware (**D**, **E**, **F**).

CONTINUED

A
B
C
D
E
F

G
BEYOND
PAINT
QUICK · EASY · DURABLE
ALL-IN-ONE
BONDS · PRIMES · SEALS
ONE-STEP PROCESS
NO STRIPPING
NO SANDING
FURNITURE, CABINETS,
COUNTERTOPS & MORE
H
I
J
K
L

4 If you're using standard furniture paint, sand down your surfaces. My all-in-one paint excused me from having to do any sanding (**G**)!

5 Pour your paint into your tray and get ready to roll (**H**). No, really, start rolling your first coat of paint onto your cabinet and drawer fronts (**I**)!

6 For the frames and crevices, a brush may work better since you're working in a smaller area (**J**). After your panels are fully coated, let them dry for a few hours.

7 With painter's tape, cover the walls adjacent to the frames of your cabinets and tape cabinet edges (**K**, **L**).

CONTINUED

Our kitchen was rendered off-limits during this project, but nobody complained about a weekend of takeout!

8. Roll your paint onto the frames and sides of the cabinets (**M**, **N**).
9. For the trim, use a paintbrush (**O**).
10. Once your cabinet doors and drawer fronts dry, paint a second coat (**P**).
11. Apply coats on all surfaces until opaque. This will take two to three coats (**Q**).
12. Once all surfaces are dry, put your drawer and door fronts back onto the frames.

M
N
O
P
Q
For some added color, I chose to paint the island a moody blue.

LITTLE UPGRADES

Not all DIY projects have to be days-long. I could never do my big projects back-to-back. Going to bed with an aching back and throbbing knees is a misery I can handle about once a month, but you're not going to see me start wallpapering my living room the day after I've painted my floor. So, in my downtime between major projects, it feels like a breath of fresh air to take on a quickie. I love a quick little upgrade that adds some flair without any blood, sweat, or tears. Not only do I enjoy these projects, I also think most are completely necessary to personalize your home, and I encourage you to make each of these small adjustments in your own home over time.

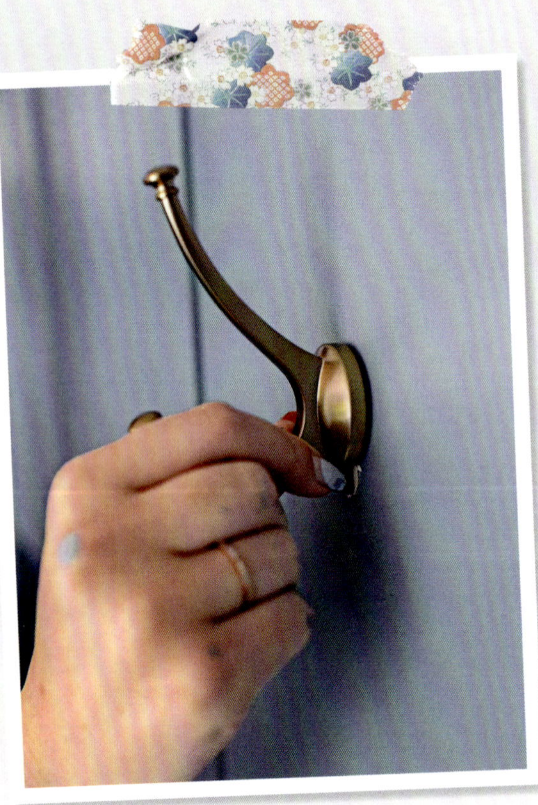

Adding under-cabinet lighting for atmosphere.

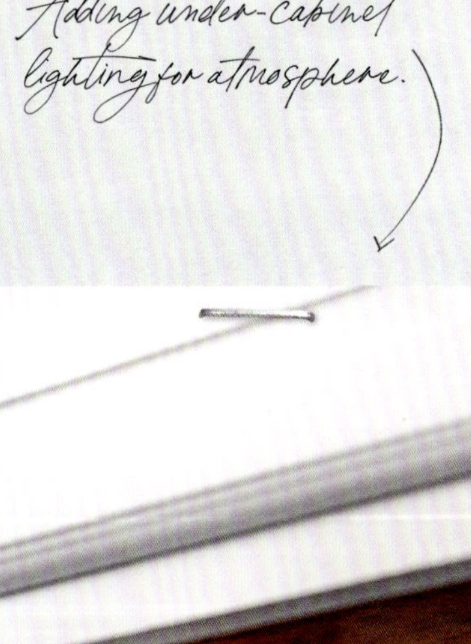

Replacing Hardware

Hardware is a decor item that is especially susceptible to trends. Right now, brass and gold are all the rage. I know I've encouraged you to avoid trends, but if you are going to get behind any of them—hardware is a good place to start. Swapping your hardware out can be a minimal-cost, minimal-time-spent change that can upgrade your kitchen—or an old piece of furniture—in less than thirty minutes.

The How-To

MATERIALS

Screwdriver

New hardware

OPTIONAL:

Putty

Putty knife

Paint

Drill

1. Remove your old hardware with a screwdriver by opening the drawer or cabinet, locating the existing screw, and twisting "lefty-loosey."
2. Keep the old screw in place if it'll fit your new hardware.
3. If you've got a fit, pop your knob or handle on the front and over the screw then "righty-tighty" your screw into the new hardware using your screwdriver.
4. If your new hardware is a different size than your existing hardware, you'll need to make new holes:
    a. Align your hardware to the door, using a level if needed. Mark where the new holes will go on your cabinets.
    b. Drill holes into the door or drawer. Fill in your old holes with putty, which you'll sand and paint over.
    c. Insert your screws through the hole and into your new hardware, twisting to get them through.

Under-Cabinet Lighting

Good lighting is the cherry on top of a luxurious-feeling room. Sometimes, while I'm watching a TV show, instead of following the plot I find myself studying the set design. Through this little habit, I learn a lot about a character through their decor. I've noticed that when wealthy characters are shown at night in their home, the lighting is simply fabulous. Lighting designers achieve this with ambient, ethereal lighting instead of overhead. A low, warm glow alights each stair riser, marking an elegant path down a stairway in the evening. Symmetrical lamps flank an expensive sofa, setting a romantic mood.

You can achieve this lighting effect without hiring an electrician or spending your yearly salary on expensive fixtures. I ordered these stick-on, battery-powered LED strips to mount underneath my kitchen cabinets. Not only does it feel luxe, but it's useful to keep them on at night. If I need a midnight snack or, more likely these days, a bottle for my baby at three in the morning, I'm able to see my way without turning on the glaring overheads.

The How-To

1. Clean underneath your cabinets very thoroughly. Lemon and vinegar cleaners are a great idea, as the acid will really fight all that grimy cooking buildup!
2. Depending on the set you bought, you'll most likely have to connect your light strips together with wires (**A**, **B**).
3. Place your peel-and-stick strips across the lighting, as well as on any hooks included that will keep the wires from drooping (**C**).
4. Attach your strips underneath your cabinets one by one (**D**).
5. Bask in your atmospheric new kitchen lighting!

Clare Rule

No big lights at night. Turn all overheads off to create a more relaxing vibe using lamps and atmospheric light.

A
B
C
D

Using Anchors

Just because our projects are *budget* doesn't mean they need to be falling apart at the seams. I want these projects to stand the test of time. That means ensuring things are done properly. Meet my friend "the anchor." He's a Taurus, so he's extremely stubborn. You can't change his mind—or sway him—no matter how much force you use! He's super possessive and won't let go of what is his. But on the positive side, he's hardworking, never slacking at his job. He's loyal, committed, and very grounded. The anchor will never let you down—unless you do him wrong. Then, watch out! He could switch on you, and all of those wonderful qualities will start backfiring. So don't screw him into the wall without using my guidelines. If you anchor your screw incorrectly, you've ruined your hopes and dreams of loyalty, commitment, and security.

I first met the anchor in my East Village apartment. I wanted to hang art, but the entire living room was brick. Pretty cool, yes! But it made decorating a challenge. For small pieces, I could nail hooks into the mortar. But I wanted to hang a gigantic framed Andy Warhol print right in the middle of the room, and it was way too heavy for any standard hook-and-nail system. So I asked my dad for help, and on his next visit from Maine, he taught me how to hang heavy art with anchors. It was a valuable lesson that I now employ often! My dad is a big "give a man a fish, you feed him for a day—teach a man to fish, you feed him for a lifetime" guy. And I'm googly eyed when he (or my father in-law, who has a whole wood workshop in his basement!) gives me a lesson on home improvement.

For this anchor tutorial, I'll be using the example of hanging the hooks in my mudroom. I could hang them directly into the wood, but I need those hooks to support the heavier things in life: my husband's work backpack, my purse (I think I need shoulder surgery), the overflowing diaper tote, and, of course, winter coats. So, I wanted to be extra careful with these, to ensure hooks don't rip off the wall, destroying my paint job while doing so.

Anchors are wonderful solutions for hanging art, hooks, or mirrors into drywall, which can easily crumble and give way without extra stability.

The How-To

MATERIALS

Screws

Drywall anchors
(make sure you buy the right size for your screws!)

Electric drill

Screwdriver

Hammer (optional)

Level (optional)

1 The most common anchors are plastic drywall anchors. I'll be using them in this tutorial, but there are other anchors for other wall types, like concrete or metal.

2 Mark the location of your screw with a pencil (**A**).

OPTIONAL: Since I needed to put two screws in the wall, I wanted to make sure they lined up correctly. Always use a level to avoid crooked lines (**B**).

3 Drill a "pilot hole" for your anchor using a drill bit that's slightly less wide than the anchor (**C**).

4 Depending on your anchor, screw or hammer it into the wall until the collar (the spiral part) sits directly next to the wall.

5 Screw your anchor into the wall all the way (**D**). You can use a drill, but I prefer a screwdriver for this part, since I want to be extra careful that the anchor goes in straight.

6 Now your anchor is ready for the screw. Place the object you're hanging over the anchor. Use your drill or screwdriver to drive the screw through the hole, stopping when it feels tight (**E**). Too much force, and you'll damage the anchor, making it unstable.

7 Your anchor will keep your screw held tight as it expands and *anchors* into the wall. Check your work by tugging on the object you mounted. It should feel stubborn.

8 Mount your item onto your screws (**F**). In my case, I used two sets of screws and anchors to hang these hooks.

A
B
STANLE
C
D
E
F

Outlet Covers

To make your room extra custom and elevated, consider purchasing outlet covers that will take your builder-grade ones to the next level. It may feel like an insignificant design contribution, but a custom cover helps add a luxurious feel to your room—it's a cherry on top that shows how considered your design truly is. Whether adorned with whimsical patterns, or colors that match your space, they introduce a touch of personality without overwhelming the room. In my opinion, *everything* in your home should be beautiful, and you don't have to sacrifice function in the process. They're just as practical and easy to clean as the standard variety. If you love the wallpaper you've hung, you can even cut out a swatch of it to match the pattern, covering your existing plate with an excess cutting. Or, to let the wallpaper shine, you can purchase glass plates with new fittings for the switches, so that the wallpaper can still be viewed behind the plate.

ABOVE: I used wallpaper samples to dress up the outlets in my upstairs hallway.

RIGHT: A gingham outlet cover I bought on Etsy to tie my son's nursery together.

Paper Blind

The morning of our final shoot for this book, I realized that I hadn't gotten around to hanging a cute curtain over the door in my entry. I had planned on creating a fabric drape, but my photographer had to leave at 11:00 A.M., and my manuscript was due to the editor that very night. Instead of shrugging my shoulders and leaving out the window treatments (that would probably have been the most sensible route), I took a trip down to the basement, where I hoard my crafts, extra decor, and things like leftover wallpaper and paint.

I was looking for a set of bamboo blinds that I thought I had some extras of. Then it occurred to me that I'd actually given them to my mom. Again, I didn't give up. I was determined to hang *something* over that door window. I saw, sticking out of a box in the corner, a few rolls of grass-cloth wallpaper. I *knew* I'd hung on to that for a reason! I had picked it up at a Habitat for Humanity store two years ago. Six rolls of beautiful, high-quality grass cloth for just ten bucks. What struck me was the textural resemblance of the wallpaper to the bamboo shade I had been searching for.

I wondered if I could make it work. So, with one hour left on the clock, I tried to create a "shade" out of this surplus wallpaper. I hadn't planned on including this craft in the book, because I assumed that whatever I ended up creating would be slapped together and nonfunctional—basically a Band-Aid window treatment I'd have to replace in a few months when I actually got my head above water.

But as I folded, pushed, cut, and hung the "blind," I started to get that thrilling feeling that something was actually working out *perfectly.* As I like to say, I believe we are most *creative* when we face *constraint;* problem-solving is the best way to invent new ideas! As I was tapping the last nail in to hang my shade, I heard my photographer's voice from over my shoulder: "Wait—I just left the room two seconds ago! Did you just MAKE THAT?!" I stepped back to look at the shade. I couldn't help but agree with her. It was pretty shocking! The shade looked great—and, best of all, it worked! It could be rolled up, rolled down, and secured with string at any height you wanted it! The top even looked legitimate.

Custom window treatments? Hundreds to thousands of dollars. My entryway window treatment? Free. Here's how to make one for yourself:

The How-To

1. Find the paper you'd like to use. Some ideas: thick, good-quality wrapping paper, extra wallpaper, painted craft paper, or even rigid fabric could work.

2. Measure your window, and cut your paper to the correct dimensions, leaving an extra 2 feet for the top and bottom details.

3. Fold back the top of your paper. Next, fold it forward, so that you can see it peaking over (A). Make one more fold forward, so that it comes around the top and forms a flap lying above the paper (B).

4. Take two strips of wood that are thin enough to be concealed by your flap. I used paint mixing sticks! Punch a hole in the middle of each using a hammer and nail. Glue your wood at the top of the paper (under the flap) (C), and poke holes in the rest of the folded paper to thread your string through (D, E).

5. Once you've gotten your string running through the wood and back flaps of paper, hang your paper above the window. Nail (or you could even Command-strip this since it's so light!) through the wood, and through the back flaps until secure to the wall above (F).

6. Conceal how the sausage was made by bringing your top flap down and gluing it over the wood and nails (G), but don't glue near the string, to make sure that the string has a clear path and can be adjusted without ungluing your paper!

7. To bring your shade up, roll the bottom of the paper toward you until you find your desired length. Tie up your string evenly to hold the rolled paper (H). Voilà! You've just made a shade!

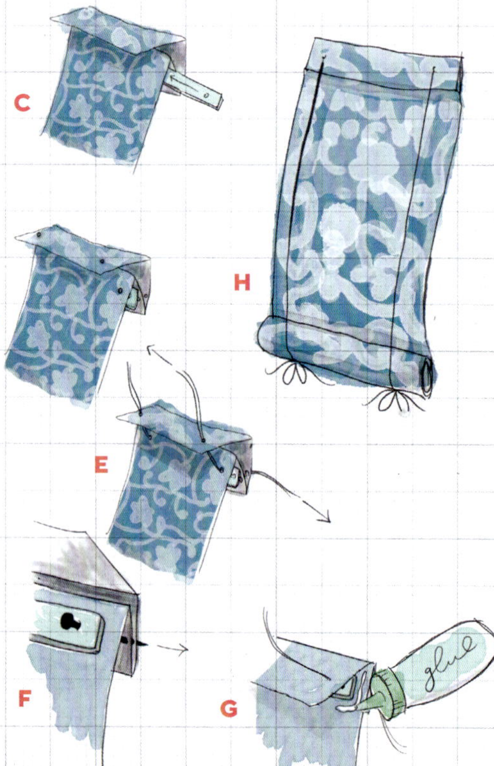

THE INTANGIBLES OF A LUXURIOUS HOME

Have you ever met a woman who gives off *luxury* without trying to? She's polished, chic, and just looks so . . . clean? Her hair is slicked back, she wears a few staple jewelry pieces, and she looks elegant in jeans and a white tee. You know she's walked into the room without even laying eyes on her, because the most beautiful and subtle scent is wafting through the space. You've asked her what she's wearing that smells so good, and she looks at you, perplexed. "I don't wear perfume!" she says, flashing you a smile and resting her manicured hand gently on your shoulder. Her breath is minty and fresh. You breathe through your nose, keeping tight lips to avoid her smelling your coffee breath. You look at her bare and glowing skin, suddenly worried that your foundation looks cakey and your hair is frizzing up. Also, you're sweating. And she looks cool as a cucumber. But instead of making you feel lesser than, she says, "I'm obsessed with your scarf. It's so unique and cool—where did you find it?" You stutter out that you found it in the clearance section at Target for $3.49, turning red when you realize she's probably never shopped for clothing at Target, let alone the clearance section. But she surprises you, parting her glossy, moisturized lips to tell you that she found a Burberry knockoff coat there last month. You watch her walk away and notice that her gait is that of a greyhound. Gentle, smooth, and slight. You curse your genetics for giving you pigeon toes and wide, inflexible hips.

Can you guess which woman I am? Well, I'll leave that to your imagination. You haven't met me in person, so you haven't witnessed the way I walk.

The luxurious woman is who I'd call an "it girl." An "it girl" achieves this status through a slew of intangible properties, from amazing scents to timeless style. You can't put your finger on her perfection—it just *is*. But though effortless she may seem, effortless she is not. You don't know about her inner workings—the two-hour evening routine of Korean skincare,

OPPOSITE: Fresh flowers will forever be my favorite luxury accessory.

the monthly aesthetician appointments. Her entire paycheck goes to lotions and shampoos that smell like roses. But, hey, at least she isn't spending money on perfume!

I'm not here to teach you how to be an "it girl"—I, for one, will never be one! This book isn't about leveling up your fashion or perfume, but it is about shaping up your home, and I want you to think about this "it girl" and her mysterious allure as a metaphor for your interior. Your home can be an "it girl" too.

It's all about those intangibles that you can't exactly put your finger on. What makes something luxurious? Yes, expensive things help. But isn't it more of a *feeling* than anything else?

When you walk into a fancy boutique, you feel transported. It's not just the beautiful cashmere folded impeccably. There's music playing. It's jazz. It puts you at ease. It's just loud enough to be noticeable. It smells so good—but you don't see a candle burning.

These intangible elements of an interior are the ones that determine a luxurious mood. Fresh flowers, well-scented natural cleaning products, intentional music, atmospheric lighting. If you want your home to exude luxury, consider these factors the cherry on top.

And listen, my house is never in perfect condition. But if I have company, I want them to feel comfortable and at ease. I want them to kick off their shoes and have an extra glass of wine with me. Most of all, I want them to come back often!

I'm guessing you picked out friends who wouldn't judge you based on the condition of your home, even if you lived in a cardboard box. If not, I think you need to find some different friends! While you want your environment to be welcoming and beautiful, you want guests to feel, above all, at ease. In order for your home to exude "it girl" qualities, remember that she doesn't wear perfume—or at least, she doesn't tell you what her scent is. So instead of the fancy-candle approach, try lighting a few unscented white pillar candles and placing them around the room to add some "glimmer." Give your surfaces a good wipe-down with naturally scented cleaning sprays. Lemon always smells fresh and uplifting. Instead of putting one large, premade floral bouquet in the middle of the table, place a few spriggy arrangements throughout your space, which will feel more carefree and less uptight. I always like to play music, and often will put vintage music videos on my TV for some added visual entertainment.

When you entertain, think of your decor as you would the drinks you serve your guests. You don't want anyone thinking you slaved over their cocktail for hours—but it should taste good! Similarily, your dinner guests shouldn't feel that you went out of your way for them to prepare for days by deep cleaning and perfecting your house. Your decor should exude comfort, joy, and a casual atmosphere for your guests.

OPPOSITE: An Easter tablescape at my house.

CHAPTER 3

FLOWERS, PLANTS, AND GREENERY

FLOWERS AND ME

One of my earliest memories is of my mom's garden. She had built out a few raised beds and filled them with vegetables. I probably remember this so well because I was terrified of the huge green worms that would crawl on her tomato plants. In the summer, she'd tend to her garden with vigor and excitement, telling me all about the different flowers, vegetables, and herbs. If I close my eyes, I can vividly remember the smell of her thyme plant and feel the delicate leaves as she held my tiny hand out to touch them.

When I was in my early twenties, I was nursing hangovers and quitting jobs left and right. I couldn't even keep a succulent alive in my apartment. Conversely, in her twenties, my mom had two little kids, two dogs, the occasional bunny, and was designing a new-build house with zero experience. Plus, she had become an avid gardener in her early twenties, and by thirty she was a total pro. She even went back to school to take horticultural design courses in her forties. My mom knows the Latin name for any tree, shrub, and especially perennial plant that she encounters. Perennials are her specialty—our garden was filled with hydrangeas, roses, and what felt like a million other

LEFT: A tropical arrangement for my wedding.

ABOVE: Pink roses are the *most* luxurious.

MASON

plants I couldn't pronounce the names of. I think that for my mom, as for many of your own mothers, gardening was second nature. She was raised by my Nana, whose vegetable gardens fed their family of six all summer long.

Thanks to the exposure my mom provided me, I came to appreciate the beauty of flowers from a young age. I loved picking flowers in our backyard to create arrangements. Looking back, I probably picked a lot of weeds! She taught me that fairies were *definitely* real and helped me build houses for them out of moss and twigs. She'd leave gifts for me in the fairy houses overnight, so that when I woke up, I was delighted to find what the fairies gave me. Acorn top? No, honey. That's a *fairy hat*. Mushrooms were their umbrellas, and flowers were their best friends.

My favorite childhood song went: *"Spring is here," said the bumblebee. "How do you know?" asked the old oak tree. "I just saw a daffodil, dancing with a fairy on a windy hill."* At night, she'd read me Cicely Mary Barker's *Complete Book of the Flower Fairies*. I'd cuddle into her, looking at the beautiful illustrations of fairies next to their assigned flower.

Another early memory of mine is of my Mimi (Dad's mother). She was a fabulous woman who sported bright pink lipstick, an ever-styled coif of white hair, and Chanel ballet flats with miniskirts until her final years. Though Mimi was ever-chic during the week, as she ran her own boutique, on the weekends she sported a flannel shirt with athletic shorts and woke up early to spend the daylight hours perfecting her garden. Unlike my mom, who focused primarily on perennials, Mimi used lots of annuals in her summer garden. Each spring, when she'd arrive back in Maine from wintering in Florida, one of the first things she'd do was drive over to the greenhouse to buy her pansies, petunias, and violas. I often marched along behind her, observing her each and every move, as she sorted through shades of yellow to find the perfect daffodils.

OPPOSITE: Ranunculus from my cutting garden, defying gravity with the help of a flower frog placed at the bottom of their vase.

ABOVE: My mom, helping me out with a DIY project.

Mimi's garden was an explosion of color. My favorite of her blooms were her beach roses, which lined the garden fence, exuding the most heavenly scent. She laid down rocks engraved with sayings on them and hung wooden signs from her fence. The saying I remember most is one she'd even exclaim aloud often: *Always stop and smell the roses.* Mimi was constantly bent over on a green cushion in her garden, ripping out weeds and trimming

back shrubs. She took her weekend job as avid gardener just as seriously as her weekday role as boss of her company.

Mimi taught me that you can successfully run your own business while also relaxing to enjoy the things you love most. Without a doubt, flowers were one of her greatest joys in life. And thanks to the women in my family, they've become one of mine, too. I'm no gardening expert, and my thumb isn't green yet. But I've spent the past two years in my own garden, trying to whip it into shape.

House hunting was an exhaustive and upsetting process. Not only were we moving out of the city we called home for seven years, but we realized that our dream of a big house and a big yard just wasn't possible given our budget. The homes we viewed were lackluster at best, and most of them had glaring issues, like the one sitting directly next to the highway, or the one that flooded each spring. We had just about given up when my realtor called, asking if we were free to see a house that very night. My husband and I were driving up to Maine from New York City, and she'd called at the right time. We were just crossing the border into Connecticut and were able to pull off to see the house.

I kept my lips sealed to make sure my husband could give his own unbiased thoughts, but I immediately knew that house was ours before even walking into the front door. I didn't care what lay beyond the entryway—whether it was carpeted bathrooms or rotting wood—because I needed to buy this house. Why? Why, for the hydrangeas, of course! The house was small

OPPOSITE: Hydrangeas cut from the bushes at my house.
ABOVE: Echinacea from my garden, at the height of their beauty in June.

and well-kept, flanked with seven gargantuan hydrangea bushes that were sporting flowers bigger than my head. There were hydrangeas of the limelight variety, reaching toward the sun and taller than my six-foot-four husband. Shorter bushes exploded with pink, purple, and blue flowers. I was sold.

Thankfully, the house was in decent condition after a renovation in the nineties, and it checked all of our boxes. You can't imagine my utter glee when my husband begrudgingly admitted it was perfect (we were moving out of the city per *my* wishes, and I had to practically drag him by the collar to convince him to move to Connecticut). That same weekend, we took the house, and its beautiful hydrangeas, off the market.

As part of our closing deal, the previous homeowners included six months of free landscaping by the company they employed. I had expected to be doing all gardening and yard work on my own, so this was great news to my inexperienced self. The landscapers were great—they took care of weeds, cut our grass, and had our yard looking more manicured than it ever will look again. But one chilly morning in October, I accidentally slept in. I was pregnant and didn't know it, so understand that utter exhaustion and hormone overload contribute to the reaction I'm about to describe. I walked downstairs expecting to look out the window and see my hydrangeas, which were still somehow in bloom and turning

beautiful shades of mauve. Instead, I saw barren stumps of wood, all leaves and blossoms raked away into a landscaping truck that had pulled out of my driveway hours before.

I ran outside and immediately broke down into tears. Did the landscapers hate me? Where were all my hydrangea flowers? I wept on my front steps and, after collecting myself, called my mom. She told me that you have to cut hydrangeas back every year to ensure they grow back beautifully in the spring and summer. I was flabbergasted.

I still couldn't shake just how *far* back they'd been cut. How on earth could they regrow to become as large as they were before? They'd have to grow 5 feet in total to achieve the same robust size as they were when I first visited the house. I tried to put it out of my mind, as I had other things to worry about. A few days later, I found out that hydrangeas weren't going to be my focus in the summer—we would have a BABY by then! After the landscaping company's free term expired, I got to gardening myself. I was determined to bring my baby home to a garden full of flowers in June. I'd already planted fifty tulip bulbs in the ground that fall, and impatiently waited until the end of April to buy rosebushes, holly hedges, lilies, lupine, phlox, veronica, ornamental onion, zinnia, and many other perennials, focusing on ones that would bloom early in time for my son's arrival.

While I was busy digging up earth and planting new flowers, I wasn't noticing the subtle yet consistent new growth my hydrangea bushes were putting out. It wasn't until my baby shower that I realized they'd made almost a three-quarters recovery from their stumpy condition. But I was skeptical they'd be back to their old selves by the time I gave birth.

I'd been in the hospital for almost a week after giving birth early due to preeclampsia, and when we finally arrived home with the baby and pulled into the driveway, my heart soared. My tulips had bloomed, the lawn was green, the lilac bush had popped and the hydrangeas were back to their gargantuan size. We carried our son through the garden before entering the house. He was premature and slept about twenty-two hours a day, so his eyes weren't open, but I felt such overwhelming gratitude and joy that I could walk my baby through the garden. Not only were we both alive and healthy after a traumatic week, but my hydrangeas were, too.

FLOWER ARRANGEMENTS

A luxurious home must have flowers. Fresh bouquets exude sophistication and romance. But since you're reading this book, I'm guessing you don't want to spend lots of money on beautiful arrangements at the florist each week. A good-size professional bouquet can cost upward of $150, and that's a LOT to spend on something that will unavoidably wilt and die within two weeks. Even the premade bouquets at grocery stores could drain your shopping allowance for the week.

Instead, you can save lots of money by making your own arrangements. It's really not as prohibitive as you may think—florist experience is not necessary if you take my advice! I buy my flowers at the grocery store, where they're affordable if you buy them by *type* of flower instead of in a premade arrangement. For example, a mixed bouquet with blue hydrangeas could be around $36. But to purchase a sleeve of blue hydrangeas, you could spend as little as $6. Then you could select a couple more types of flowers and keep it well under $25!

With this method, you get more bang for your buck. I always make multiple arrangements when I get home from the store. I'll use two-thirds of the florals for a hefty arrangement that usually sits on my kitchen island, then make two smaller arrangements with the rest, putting one in the bedroom and one in the living room.

One staple I don't buy—which may surprise you—is filler. Though I love eucalyptus and green dragon, I choose to skip the cost of filler. To me, it's just that—*filler*. Instead, I spend money on more showstopping flowers and keep the top leaves on to add volume where needed. Shop in threes. The perfect bouquet can be made up of just three types of flowers, as long as you vary them in scale:

RECIPE FOR A PERFECT BOUQUET

FROM THE KITCHEN OF: Clare Sullivan

SHOP IN THREES

1. **SELECT ONE TYPE OF BIG AND BOLD FLOWER,** such as hydrangea, peony, or gerbera daisy. This flower will serve as the star of your bouquet.
2. **SELECT A SECONDARY, MIDSIZED FLOWER** such as rose, ranunculus, zinnia, or dahlia, in a new color that won't compete with your star flower.
3. **PICK A SMALL, SPRIGGY STEMMED FLORAL** to add height and scale variety. This could be something like stock, thistle, sweet pea, or snapdragon.

SINGLE FLOWER ARRANGEMENTS

I love an arrangement using just one type of flower. When flowers are given the chance to speak for themselves, it's a beautiful thing.

Here are some flowers that look excellent on their own:

- Tulip
- Hydrangea
- Dahlia
- Ranunculus
- Rose
- Peony

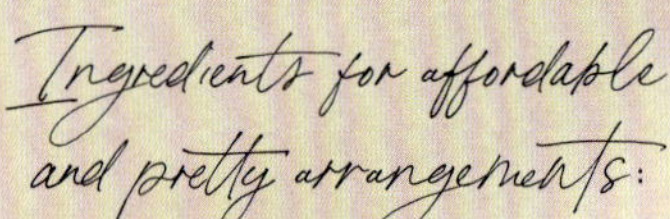

Joyful Spring for $20

Summer Tones for $18

Remember to vary your stem height for visual interest.

A sophisticated bouquet includes a variety of scales, from small spray roses to big fluffy ones!

KEEPING YOUR FLOWERS ALIVE

There's nothing more disappointing than waking up to flowers that have wilted after just a few days. To keep your flowers fresh and beautiful for a week or more, I recommend changing their water every other day and trimming the stems at a 45-degree angle often to ensure the flowers are drinking clean, bacteria-free water. Freshly cut stems help flowers absorb the water they need to thrive.

Bacteria is a cut flower's archnemesis. To avoid bacterial growth, remove any leaves or blossoms below water level. Clean stems will perform much better if leaves aren't feeding bacterial growth!

Flower food is another excellent way to help your flowers stay alive, but the packet from the supermarket that comes with your flowers runs out very quickly. You can make your own with basic household ingredients. All that flowers require for nutrition, aside from water, is acid and sugar. Try this out the next time you want to extend the life of your bouquet:

Basic Flower Food Recipe:
one part lemon juice, one part vinegar, and two parts sugar.

OPPOSITE: Trim your stems every couple days to keep your bouquet fresh.
ABOVE: Removing leaves prevents bacteria from forming under the waterline.

WORKING WITH HYDRANGEAS

Hydrangeas are beautiful flowers, reminiscent of the coastal Northeast. They feel like salt air, a blue-and-white striped T-shirt, and classic New England summertime. They're reliable while growing wild in the garden but can be trouble once taken indoors. They're a highly dramatic flower and will wilt quickly in their vase if not tended to with care and knowledge. Even if you're buying cut ones at the store, you'll want to memorize this guide to all things hydrangea.

I'm so obsessed with the flowers that once I spent an entire summer day experimenting with different ways to keep them alive. I cut some already-wilted hydrangeas from my mother-in-law's garden, and she was excited to join in on the fun, being a huge hydrangea fan herself. We took three different recommendations that I found on the internet and experimented by cutting each stem at a 45-degree angle, making sure that no flower had an upper hand. Here were our results:

1. **VODKA:** adding a shot glass of vodka to the water.
   Result: A-
2. **ASPIRIN:** Crushing up a tablet of aspirin and sprinkling in.
   Result: A
3. **COLD WATER:** Soaking the blossoms in cold water:
   Result: A+

LEFT: Hydrangea, a highly sensitive flower, can be reinvigorated in a bath of cold water, which will rehydrate her blossoms to restore a lively and full look.

ABOVE: Shaving off the ends of the stem to increase water intake, which will help these hydrangeas last longer in a vase.

LEFT: A weeks-old hydrangea holding her color beautifully after drying in a vase.

While each method worked wonders, our clear winner was the one I least expected! Soaking the wilted flower in cold water led to the fastest and most awe-inspiring recovery. To try it yourself, fill a cup (or bowl if you're dealing with multiple wilted blooms and need extra space) with cold water from the tap. Submerge your hydrangeas head-down into the water and leave them for a few hours. Mine perked up completely in about three hours.

To prepare your hydrangeas for captive vase life, shave the ends of each stem. You can shave the ends using an open pair of scissors or a sharp knife. Angle your blade, shaving downward and focusing on the bottom few inches of the stem. This goes for any "woody" flower. Because of their bark, they struggle to absorb as much water as a more porous flower stem would. Peeling back rough layers at the bottom of the stem ensures they'll be able to drink like a fish! Next, remove all leaves below the water line so that they don't grow bacteria in your vase water.

Hydrangeas are the absolute best when it comes to dried arrangements. Something about their papery petals allows them to bite the dust without succumbing to the decay that we, and other flowers, face after death. Sorry for getting morbid, but it's pretty amazing how these flowers can hold their own, even as ghosts of their past selves!

To dry them, I use two different methods. They work equally well, and I don't prefer one over the other, but once my basement rafters are full of dried, hanging flowers, I'll switch to doing it in vases. Or vice versa—this fall, I didn't have one vase in my whole house that was unoccupied by drying hydrangea bouquets! I even filled my entire bathtub when I ran out of room. For either method, cut hydrangeas in late summer or early fall when the petals feel papery and dry. Avoid those still in their peak, as they should continue flourishing in your garden, and won't do well since they're too moist at that point to dry. To cut the stems, use sharp scissors or pruning shears, keeping the stems as long as possible without cutting too low on the plant, which could restrict next year's growth. Remove all the leaves—unlike the flowers, these aren't as pretty when dry.

Over the span of about two to four weeks, you'll see their colors fading into vintage tones like mauve, olive, gray-blue, or burgundy. When they feel completely dry, they're ready for display!

Their pillowy blue blooms put hydrangeas in the running as my favorite flower.

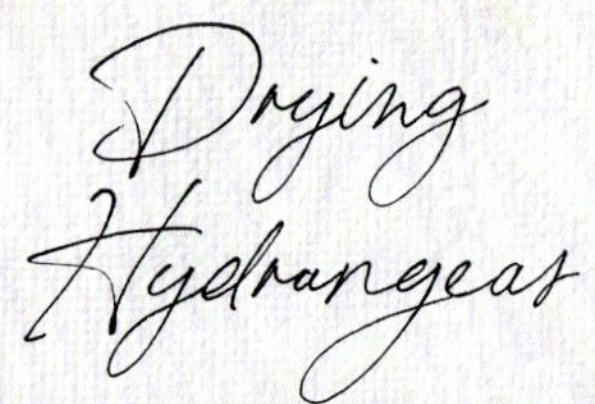

METHOD 1

HANGING TO DRY: Group up to ten stems together with a rubber band or string. Find a room that's dry and dark, like a basement, closet, or attic. Hang your arrangements upside down. Keep your bundles spaced out nicely to ensure they have enough breathing room to dry beautifully.

METHOD 2

DRYING IN A VASE: Pour one to two inches of water into your vase. With this method, the water evaporates slowly, so the flowers can dry evenly. Place your hydrangeas in the vase, making sure each stem touches the water. Make sure each flower has breathing room to avoid mold. Place your vase out of direct sunlight, and don't worry about them! Do not refill the water as it evaporates. The slow absorption and evaporation process helps the flowers maintain their shape and color.

PERFECT ROSES

If you've ever come home from the store, put your flowers in a vase, and called it a day . . . you've committed a major floral-arranging sin. I know you're busy, you're tired, you're fed up with everything and everyone around you, but you'll enjoy those flowers so much more if you take a few minutes to cut the stems. When you buy flowers, the stems are long and equal in length. Thus, when unwrapped and placed directly into a vase, they sprawl out in an unfashionable display. In my opinion, shorter arrangements always look more tidy and professional, especially if you're using just one type of flower, or not working with a ton of blooms. Take a look at the before-and-after on page 182, where I demonstrate what roses look like when untrimmed versus trimmed.

Roses, the flower of romance, are a favorite of mine. I prefer the squat, loose garden rose to the more standard, taller "Valentine's Day" rose. But the best thing about all roses is that you can sculpt them to your liking!

To expose more of your rose's beautiful petals, roll the stem between your hands. Be careful not to get stabbed by a thorn! Quickly rotate the stem between your palms, and watch as the rose transforms like a ballerina's spinning tutu. If you lose a petal, that's your sign to stop! Roses can handle some spinning, but be careful not to go overboard. Too much spinning could cause severe petal loss!

The next step is to remove your leaves. Sometimes leaves add character, but I'm going for a polished bouquet in which the roses shine independent of any distraction. After you peel

the leaves off, remove any brown petals on the outside of the flowers.

Next, you're going to master the art of European Hand Arranging. Sounds fancy, but it's super intuitive. Essentially, you're creating a spiral with your stems. Start with one rose in your hand and lay a second one diagonally across it, so that the stems create an X. Rotate your hand slightly and place the next rose, crossing the stem at the X. Each stem should run on a diagonal. Keep consistently rotating your bouquet as you add roses pointed at the same angle. Once you've finished, you'll be grasping a rounded bouquet of roses with their stems perfectly spiraled around one point! This looks beautiful in a clear vase, and helps the roses stay in place.

Eye the height of your vase and trim the stems so that the roses will just clear the top of it. We're looking for a full, rotund arrangement without gaps or stems showing!

Place your roses into their new home, and admire your beautiful arrangement, adjusting any roses that seem too high or low.

A few adjustments can make a huge difference in the appearance of your bouquet.

Rose Spinning

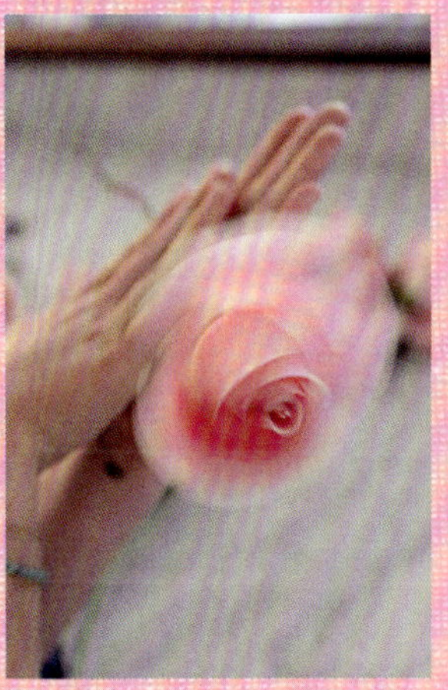

Look at how a couple of spins turn this closed-up lady into a free and graceful ballerina!

Hand Arranging

Reflexing the outer leaves by turning them "inside out" creates a fluffier-looking rose.

YOUR OWN LITTLE INDOOR HERB GARDEN

Elegant people don't cook with dried, jarred spices. At least that's how I imagine it—they either have the time to pick up fresh herbs from the farmers market or pick their own from their acre-long garden. So, here's my solution for fresh herbs when you don't have the outdoor space or time in your day!

A pot filled with fresh herbs makes cooking a more enjoyable experience, and it doesn't hurt to look at, either.

A
B
C
D
E
F
G

The How-To

MATERIALS

Self-draining pot

Soil

Herbs like rosemary, thyme, sage, and basil

Rocks

Permanent marker

LEARN FROM MY MISTAKE: Group herbs with similar characteristics into your pot. I put basil, which needs lots of water, with rosemary, which doesn't! Thus my indoor garden didn't last as long as I had hoped.

1. Fill your pot up with soil and create divots for your herbs to go into (**A**).
2. Once your pot is filled with soil, take your herbs out of their containers (**B**).
3. From the bottom, loosen their roots until the growth system looks free of its strangled cube shape (**C**, **D**).
4. Plant your herb into the pot, making sure that the base of the plant is covered with soil (**E**).
5. Add the rest of your herbs, making sure they have plenty of breathing room (**F**). Pat down the soil (**G**), and water them in generously to welcome them home!
6. I made labels for each herb using rocks I found in my yard and writing their names with a paint pen (see page 189).

THYME
ROSEMAR

THE TAPE TRICK

It's incredibly frustrating when your flowers don't listen. Although I consider myself a flower-whisperer, I cannot get them to cooperate with me when it comes to staying in place in their vase! So, for years I've been turning to "the tape trick."

Any tape will get the job done, but I prefer the near-invisible look of gift-wrapping tape. Tape a line from one side of your vase to the other. Continue taping to create a grid, with small holes in between pieces of tape.

Insert your stems into the holes, putting taller flowers in the middle and shorter ones around the edges of your vase.

WECK

A METAL FLORAL frog is a smart way to keep your flowers standing up straight. Place it at the bottom of your vase and stick stems throughout the pins. It's like sculpting a beautiful floral statue—you're fully in control of where the flowers stand.

BUDGET LUXURY VASES

I love to collect beautiful vases. I have some interesting ones: a Dutch tulipiere with multiple spouts that display individual tulips, a gigantic blown-glass cylinder that's bigger than my son, and even a glass "shopping bag" that holds water and flowers. But I find that my go-to vases are the simplest ones. And nothing does the job better than a simple mason jar. It holds enough water for a midsize arrangement, and tapers enough at the top to hold the stems up. When you're resourceful enough, any vessel can become a vase. For a while, I was addicted to those French yogurts in the blue ceramic containers. I'm not sure if it was the taste of the yogurt, or the fact that I was getting a free jar with each afternoon snack that kept me going back for them. Like many of my hyper-fixations, the yogurt one passed quickly, but the jars certainly stayed. I use them for bud arrangements on my windowsill! Even a peanut butter jar, if scrubbed down and run through the dishwasher, can make for a great vase. These free vases are especially useful to have around if you ever make arrangements to give out as gifts. Tie a ribbon at the top of your jar, and you've got a professional-looking bouquet for a friend!

A vase is a vase isn't a vase: Have fun with swapping out a boring vase for something more fun. I love how the orange in this vintage fresh coffee cup is played up by the brightly colored chrysanthemum it holds.

I LOVE FILLING a window ledge with bud vases. These zinnias, grown in my friend's garden, each get their own moment in the sun. Flowers with interesting, curved, strong stems like zinnias, ranunculus, or dahlias work best. For bud vases, get resourceful by using yogurt jars, glass bottles, or even small candle containers that have burned to the bottom.

A SEASONAL BOUQUET

OPPOSITE: A Christmas celebration of gerbera daisy, rose, hypericum, veronica, and the strangely prehistoric—yet visually delightful—protea.

TOP LEFT: Red hypericum adds a festive touch in holiday arrangements.

TOP RIGHT: Gerbera daisies are certainly a showstopping flower. I leave florist supports on the stems for stability, but make sure they're camouflaged by other flowers.

RIGHT: Mix it up: Make sure your flowers are varied in size, color, and appearance to create a dynamic bouquet.

IVING MY
BEST LIFE
STOP AND
SMELL
ROSES
NOUVEAU RI
IS BETTER THA
NO RICHE AT A
You get what you get
and you don't pitch a fit
WHAT A TI
TO BE ALIV
BOUGHT
IS FINE
Shopping
FOR YEARS
AND STILL
HAVE Nothing
TO WEAR

CHAPTER 4

COLLECTING, CURATING, AND CREATING YOUR DREAM HOME

Duchess
HONEY BUNS
12 Packs
27

THE THRILL OF THE HUNT

I wasn't raised religious, though I was raised to hold one religious credo about Sundays: They should be spent antiquing. Back when I was a freckled, tomboy version of myself, my dad would wake me up early and we'd jump into whatever vintage beater he was driving that summer. I never had to wonder where we were headed, because our destination was always the same: the flea market in Arundel, Maine.

Many of the sellers knew me by name, and I was fascinated with them. There was the Fi Dollah guy, who'd croon as you walked by: "Everything's fi dollahs today folks! Fi dollahs!" There was Howie, my dad's friend who's since passed. Howie sold a bit of everything, and always at a low price. Vicky was my favorite, since she waited tables at the Captain's Restaurant down the street from our house, and sold a variety of vintage Breyer horse toys, which were the first items I "collected."

As I got older, I spent less time antiquing with my dad. I found it embarrassing that our house was chock-full of dusty old stuff, and wished that our crowded home looked more like the modern, clean houses that my friends lived in. I'd roll my eyes when my dad came home on Saturday with a pile of nautical antiques, and vowed that when I grew up, my house would be "junk-free."

But after regretfully shunning my dad and his antiquing habit during my high school years, something happened to me in college. I realized that I loved history—so much so that I chose it as my major. I became interested in the Victorians and their strange clothing, flipped through images of Louis XIV's ornate interiors with awe, and developed an obsession with American Impressionist painting. My interest in history sparked a renewed curiosity about "old shit." And on college breaks, I started accompanying my dad on his antiquing jaunts again.

OPPOSITE: Catching up with Vicky at her table. **ABOVE:** My dad, smiling at me with pride as he shows off the lemon-gold mirror he bought that morning.

My dad worked long hours, so I looked forward to spending time with him on the weekends, even if it meant following him around flea markets all day long.

After graduation, my reinvigorated interest in antiques would help me find cheap furniture and decor that I could use in my New York apartment. I realized that it's much better to buy vintage than to shop at new-furniture stores. Plus, an IKEA unit withers in comparison to the quality of an eighteenth-century dresser! I remember buying my first piece of original art at an estate sale. It was just three dollars, but totally beautiful—it still hangs in my house today!

And now, not only am I totally addicted to "the thrill of the hunt," but I've also improved my relationship with my dad immensely. We have an unbreakable bond, and the time we spend together antiquing has solidified it.

I will, however, transparently admit that while we don't argue as vehemently as we did when I was in high school, we do tend to get a little cutthroat when it comes to the items we collect. My dad will make sure that nobody wakes up as he sneaks out of the house on weekend mornings, arriving at the flea at 6 A.M. to scour the tables for nautical antiques. When I arrive a couple hours later, he'll still be perusing the alleys, holding anything from shell boxes to chinoiserie. I don't think he even likes this stuff, but he certainly knows *I do,* which is reason enough for him to take it off the market. If I'm lucky, he'll give me a vase or a plate. But most days, I end up angrily protesting his competitive nature, demanding he stop buying all my favorite stuff before I get the chance to even see it. I guess I'm gonna have to start waking up earlier.

Now that I'm a parent, I know how much my dad must have loved my little-kid enthusiasm about the flea market. I'm sure that I provided some joy to him by tagging along on his thrifting adventures. I hope my own son will want to go antiquing with me, but if he doesn't, it's an activity I've come to love doing on my own. It's great to go thrifting with a friend, but when I'm on a mission to find affordable home goods,

ABOVE: Hand-embroidered napkins will make a great gift for my chicken-loving friend.

RIGHT: Flea markets are a glassware lover's heaven.

BELOW: You never know what you'll find.

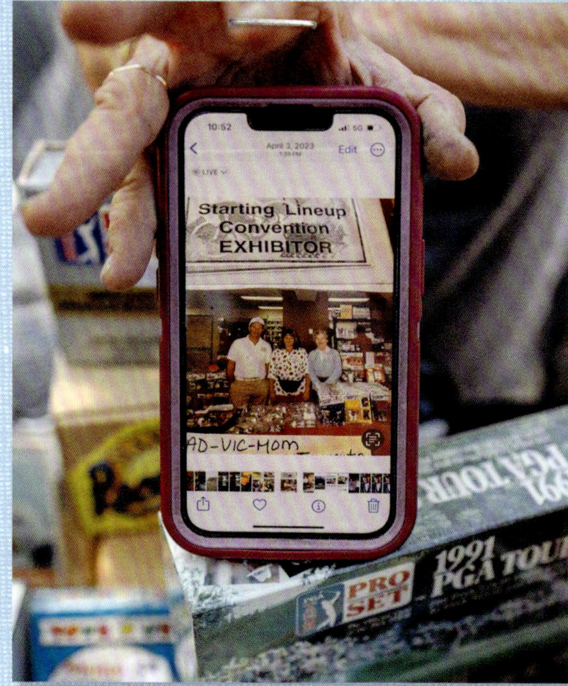

Starting Lineup
Convention
EXHIBITOR
AD-VIC-Mom
PRO SET
1991 PGA TOUR

OPPOSITE TOP AND LEFT: Vicky Lush has been selling antiques since 1986, and now most of her inventory is from clearing out her parents' house.

OPPOSITE RIGHT: Antiquing runs in the blood: a picture of Vicky with her parents at an antiques convention.

RIGHT: Curt Nixon has been selling antiques for eight years, but he always was a collector. Most of his items are from his personal collection, and his income from the flea market helps him in retirement. He makes the lengthy trip to the flea all the way from New Hampshire.

ABOVE: Alfred Martell sells at the flea once a week, and had his own antique store called Halfway Antiques. Over the years, he's amassed quite the collection of goods; he sources his products by perusing yard and estate sales. His favorite item to collect? Toothpick holders: "I have cabinets full of them." When I asked how many he owned, he estimated more than one thousand. Alfred has witnessed his generation and those before him age out of the antiques business: They've passed away or become sick. He's fearful for the future of the industry and hopes that younger generations will show an interest. I assured him that there are plenty of us who love antiquing, and I hope he'll see more and more millennials, Gen Zers, and even Gen Alphas showing up to the flea over the next few summers.

I get utterly lost in the thrill of the hunt. It's meditative, fun, and all-immersing. I encourage you to spend a Sunday hitting up antiques stores or find the flea market closest to you.

Just last week, I headed to Mongers Market in Bridgeport, Connecticut. On our drive up, I spoke my intentions aloud: "Universe, please bless me with something fabulous today. I'm confident we'll find something beautiful for our house."

My husband rolled his eyes, and I gave him a knowing look. He begrudgingly began stating his own manifestation—that he'd find something he needed.

I've learned over the years that you can't go thrifting with an agenda. If you're looking for a 40-inch walnut console table, I can almost guarantee you won't find it that afternoon. So instead of looking for specific items, I like to keep an open mind and follow my taste. It's more fun to be surprised, anyway.

As luck would have it, that afternoon we found two matching lamps. They were jade-green porcelain with pebbled details and decent shades. They actually turned on, too! Even better, the pair was priced at under $150 (if you're a seasoned antiquer, you know that pairs of good lamps are wildly expensive—like, $400 and up in nicer vintage shops). I also found an ancient wrought-iron bench that had been newly reupholstered with beautiful designer fabric.

The lamps and bench answered our manifestations in every way: fabulous, beautiful, and definitely needed! We had two unoccupied side tables in our dimly lit living room for the lamps to provide some illumination.

So, when you're off antiquing, remember to save room in your tote bag for surprises. And though I want you going in with an open mind, I do have a few tips that'll help you have a productive day "junking."

Before buying anything old *and* electric, always check if it works!

OPPOSITE: Thrifted finds for the nursery.

Hers
Ball
PERFECT
MASON

MAXIMIZING YOUR DAY AT THE FLEA— A GUIDE

1. **BE FRIENDLY TO SELLERS.** People who sell antiques are usually a little crazy—in the best way. They've chosen an unorthodox, inconvenient, and truly wild way to make a living—which makes them super cool. I've heard stories that make my jaw drop: This summer, a jewelry dealer told me about how he changed his life for the better after an encounter with the Virgin Mary. It's always a good day at the flea when you've walked away with a new friend. Also, a smile doesn't hurt when trying to negotiate a lower price on some vintage glassware.

2. **IT'S ALL ABOUT WHO YOU KNOW.** If you meet a friendly seller who sells items you love, tell them what you're on the hunt for. I give out my number and make sure that in the contact, the seller writes what to text me about when they find it—for example: "Clare—vintage jewelry boxes."

3. **ASK QUESTIONS.** Before you buy something, it's important to know its provenance so that you're confident with the amount of cash you're about to fork over. Is it actually antique? Was it owned by Judy Garland? If you don't ask, you may never know!

OPPOSITE: My finds from a Saturday morning spent at the flea.

RIGHT: Always carry a tote with extra room for treasures!

4. **DON'T BE INTIMIDATED BY LARGE ITEMS.** Even if you arrived at the flea in a tiny car, or by bike, you could still purchase large items and furniture. Often sellers have trucks, and if they don't, they'll know a guy who can deliver your item for you. It may cost extra.

5. **DO A BRISK WALKTHROUGH** before taking a closer look at the different tables. That way, if there's something incredible, it'll catch your eye on the first pass and you can snatch it up. But if not, you can then take a closer look at items while you make a second, slower round.

6. **YOU KNOW WHAT THEY SAY ABOUT CASH.** It's king! Some sellers take online payment, but most still require cash. Give yourself a budget and take out your money. If you need to get more, sellers will put an item on hold for you while you run to the ATM.

7. **YOU CAN NEGOTIATE, BUT DON'T INSULT!** At flea markets, sellers often sell their items for way below market value. Flea markets are where antique shop owners and online resellers go for "wholesale prices." Often you'll be able to knock $5 or $10 off the price, but make sure not to take advantage of a seller's kindness. I, for one, need the flea market economy to keep on keepin' on. It's a dying industry, but I have confidence that an influx of younger people will help bolster it as a stalwart of Americana.

8. **A PRO TIP FROM MY DAD,** who reigns supreme when it comes to scoring deals and making educated purchases, is to clandestinely look on your phone to compare prices while shopping. Do a quick Google search to find the item, or comparable items, listed for sale online. Even better, head to eBay, where you can look up items that have actually been sold. There's often a huge difference between an item's listed price and what it actually *sold* for. You're aiming for the latter.

RESERVED
VOLVO
240
PARKING
ONLY
ALL OTHERS WILL
BE SOLD FOR SCRAP

Seth Thomas
NORGE

Great
Mini
24-
4-

Right at Home
VINTAGE ROSES
My pièce de résistance, the "shmantel."

DISPLAYING YOUR COLLECTIONS

Our female ancestors were hunter-gatherers. It's in our DNA to gather up stuff we like, and hunt for things we want! As I've already shared with you, I am a hunter-gatherer of antiques. But it doesn't stop there! I won't get into all of my neurodivergent hyper-fixations. (Two words: Hello Kitty.) I will, however, share with you that I'm a hunter-gatherer of shells.

I've always collected stuff. In fourth grade, I started an eraser-collecting club. Oh, you think that's dumb? Well, it was the coolest club to be a member of in 2004. At the beach, I'd pocket rocks that were extra shiny. I picked pieces of mica, a reflective and flaky mineral, out of our driveway. I'm sure that you, too, have memories of filling your pockets with things you saw and liked. Hopefully not at the candy store or from a boutique. That's stealing. We're not talking about stealing, here. No, no. This is *collecting.*

I really like walking on the beach. If you haven't picked up on this yet, I'm not very good at relaxing. It's hard for me to sleep at night, or to even get relaxed enough to sit through a thirty-minute television episode. It drives my husband CRAZY! But for some reason, I'm able to relax when I walk the beach. I can't *sit* at the beach—that's for crazy people like my uncle Brian, who has enough control over his impulsivities to sit and relax at the beach every day during the summer. Yep, every day. I wish

OPPOSITE: My pièce de résistance, the "shmantel." **ABOVE, TOP:** I take shelling very seriously. **ABOVE, BOTTOM:** Some days, Mother Nature can be very generous with the gifts she washes up to shore for you.

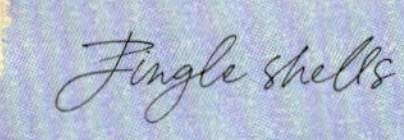
Jingle shells

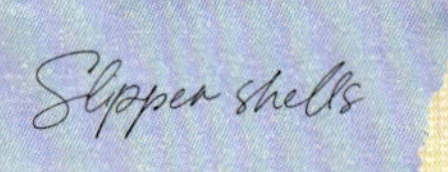
Slipper shells

I could be more like him, but at least I can feel relaxed while *walking* the beach.

I think the only reason I can withstand the monotony of a relaxing beach walk is that it's so much more than a walk. It's actually a *hunt*. I'm like a dog without her bone, scurrying from tide pool to tide pool with one objective in mind: pick. up. shells.

I treat it like a game. Your basic slipper shell, which is a dime a dozen here in the Northeast, counts as one measly point. Jingle shells, or *Anomia* for the beach nerds out there, are worth five. Here's where things get interesting. Scallops get me a whopping ten points, and angel shells are worth a staggering fifteen points. I don't actually know the real name for those angel shells, but they look like wings, so I stick to it. A good beach walk will get me to more than one hundred points. If I get my husband to tag along, he's good for another seventy-five, on average.

But don't think I'll drop my panties for any old shell. My shelling approach is similar to how I buy antiques. There are some I value, and others I have no interest in. So, Mother Nature, don't give me "It was a big night for mussels!" I don't need 'em. And save your clams for another sheller. Now that I've filled the gaps in my shell-encrusted fireplace, I'm pickier.

I know I sound crazy. And I'm about to sound even crazier. One of my best friends, Heidi, is also a semi-professional "sheller." We are so obsessed with shells that we actually took a girls' trip to Sanibel Island, Florida, JUST to gather shells together on the beach. Heidi makes beautiful art with her shells, creating mandala patterns and framing them into gorgeous works of art!

My collections are strange, vast, and incredibly different from one another. Vintage pins, needlepoint pillows, shells, old jars, decorative plates, Hello Kitty paraphernalia, matchboxes, Adidas Gazelle sneakers, picnic baskets . . . The list goes on and will grow as my life changes.

Craft with your collections. Here I'm making a shell-covered box. In it, I may just store more shells.

Collecting can be an exploration into our nostalgia, which can be a difficult thing to face. It's easier to get back into your Beanie Baby collection than it is to deal with memories of your childhood. Sometimes it's nice to look back on the past with rose-colored glasses. Speaking of rose-colored, I found myself googling "vintage razr phone in pink 2006" the other day. What on earth would I do with an old pink cellphone? Was I finally losing my mind?! But after some reflection, it occurred to me that there's

DORAL
HOTELS AND COUNTRY CLUB
SHORE DINNERS IN DINING ROOM
LOBSTER PICNICS UNDER THE TREES
CHARLIE GROSS, Mgr.
PLAYBOY OF BOSTON
MURINE FOR YOUR EYES
SOOTHES CLEANSES
PHONE CHINA 0780
OAKE GROVE HOTEL
BOOTHBAY HARBOR
TEL. 225 · MAINE
AHWAHNEE
"HICKORY BROILED"
STEAKS AND LOBSTER
GREEN TOURANT RESTAURANT
HOTEL ROAD
AUBURN, MAINE 04210
ORA LECOMPTE, OWNER
HOTEL
TOURIST CABINS
All Modern CONVENIENCES
SKIERS
SWIMMING RIDING
Blackwater Falls State Park
Davis, West Virginia
Phone 259-3216
OPEN ALL YEAR
TEL. 1440
HAYES' DINER
All Conveniences
783-8576
AUBURN, MAINE
PLEASES US

I know who I am,
because I can see it in front of me.

OPPOSITE: Old matchboxes tell stories of establishments come and gone.

ABOVE: A sampling of antique platters hung in my living room.

usually a deeper meaning behind our desire to *collect*. Perhaps if we can physically attain the items that exist in our memory, we are able to feel closer to the past. Maybe there's a part of me that actually *yearns* to go back in time, when the coolest thing a gal could possess was an (what seemed like then) impossibly thin, impossibly hot-pink cellphone.

I don't think we collect nostalgia in hopes that we'll actually go back in time. But maybe we collect in the hope that we can somehow connect to our old self, the one who exists in a faraway timeline shrouded by too many emotions to go back and face. It's a nice thought, that the seven-year-old girl who loved Davy Crockett is the same woman who stores her makeup brushes in a Davy Crockett–themed vintage glass.

We collect to establish ourselves among the world of things. We're a commercialized society, which means we shop in hopes of finding happiness, and self-identify through the things we buy. I'm not here to criticize our current society, and I'm not here to praise it, either. That'd be above my pay grade. But I am here, existing within it, and participating as a member of it. I'm simply observing, and I know for a fact that collecting helps me with something that's really hard to grapple with: my understanding of *self*.

I know who I am, because I can see it in front of me. Even in the Hello Kitty figurines that I swore I wouldn't bring up in this book. But if I'm practicing what I'm preaching, to hell with it! I'll yell it from the rooftops! I love Hello Kitty! And all Sanrio characters, for that matter! Especially when they're rendered in their pre-1980 design style! And when I look at my little Hello Kitty sculpture, I think of her life's work: being kind, making friends, and spreading joy. Yes, it's a childish thing to collect. No, I don't decorate my mantel with Hello Kitty candles and Hello Kitty vases and Hello Kitty art. But Kitty is part of me, and there's no denying that. So I allow myself to store a few figurines in my bedside table.

Collect proudly, unabashedly, and enthusiastically, dear reader. And if you don't consider yourself a collector—maybe you're more of a minimalist—that's fine, too. I think you'll find that you can reflect yourself through the colors, scents, and ambience you choose for your home. But promise me that if you do see a scallop shell on the beach, you'll mail it my way? It's fifteen whole points!!

ABOVE: A collection of pins I've inherited and collected serve as fun yet useful tacks on my bulletin board.
OPPOSITE: Styling the shelves in my husband's office with his beloved collection of nautical antiques.

WANDERING WHALEMEN
AND THEIR ART:
A COLLECTION OF SCRIMSHAW MASTERPIECES
BY ALAN GRANBY
THE TEMPEST
THE MERCHANT OF VENICE
RICHARD THE SECOND
TIMON OF ATHENS
MEASURE FOR MEASURE
IAN McEWAN
ON CHESIL BEACH

Shadowboxes

Shadowboxes are a great way to display small collectibles like matchboxes, rocks, shells, or pins. Often these very special items don't get their time in the sun, because they tend to get stored in boxes or bowls. Before you start hot-gluing your objects to the board, arrange them however you want. Take a photo of the arrangement, clear your board, and reference your photo as you glue, to make sure you stick to the plan!

I've given these as gifts to my family members, and they are always well received! I think it's a wonderful way to add elegance to items that may not be expensive or exquisite—there's something very nice about elevating the appearance of items you love, even if they're not museum-worthy or made by Fabergé.

I HAVE A great love of vintage matchboxes, and even new ones—I grab them at restaurant hostess stands and buy older ones at flea markets.

Villa D'Este
RISTORANTE
Villa D'Este
RISTORANTE

Making an Impression

Making a visual impact with your collection can be tricky. To explain this next premise, I'll use pumpkins as an example. Say you've just gotten home with a trunkload of eight colorful pumpkins, and you're psyched to put them on display around your house. You put two outside the front door, one in front of the driveway, one on your kitchen counter, two flanking the garage doors, one on a bookcase, and the other next to the fireplace. Sounds like a pumpkin-palooza, right?! WRONG. I know from experience that every fall, I purchase a boatload of pumpkins, but when I get home, it feels like I barely made a decor difference. So, this Halloween, I focused my pumpkins in one location—my front steps.

By grouping the pumpkins together, I made a much grander impact than if I'd sparingly spread them around my home. Essentially, the key takeaway here is to display your collections together in one spot. It just packs a bigger punch!

You can corral items together in bowls, on trays, or even atop a stack of coffee table books. I love a collection of intaglios displayed on a mantel, or ten beautiful plates hanging together on a wall. If you've got an open surface on a console table in your living room, that's always a great place to start!

My hand-painted pumpkins grouped together on the front steps.

The
BEDSIDE
BOOK
of
BIRDS
GRAEME
GIBSON

F*CKUPS AND FIXES!

It's not that serious. It's not that serious. It's not that serious. I find myself repeating those four words to myself in the midst of most projects. Maybe I've superglued my finger to my tripod while filming a video, or even knocked a hole in my own wall. Maybe I trapped myself into a corner while painting the floor, with no way out but through. Through wet paint. *Read:* blue footprints everywhere. Maybe I even demolished half the tiles in my bathroom without realizing I'd need a pro to move the toilet before I could finish. All of these anecdotes are true, and I'm not ashamed to admit them! Nobody is perfect, and I'm about as far from it as you can get.

The goal of this book certainly is NOT for you to think I'm a master of interior-remodel projects. In fact, I hope you learn that mistakes are simply inevitable, even for someone who's made a career filming herself taking on home transformation projects. Most projects I try are ones I have no experience with. Thus most of my home projects are riddled with the inevitable mistakes that are bound to plague a trial-and-error approach. When planning a DIY project, I use Google, call family and friends who may have relevant experience, and I watch lots of YouTube videos. The problem is that everyone's home is different. A social media DIY tutorial by Bobby the Busy Builder won't always work for me, given that my own home has its own quirks. That said, my DIYs always take on a shape of their own, and I've learned to be flexible with planning them. If something goes awry, I'd

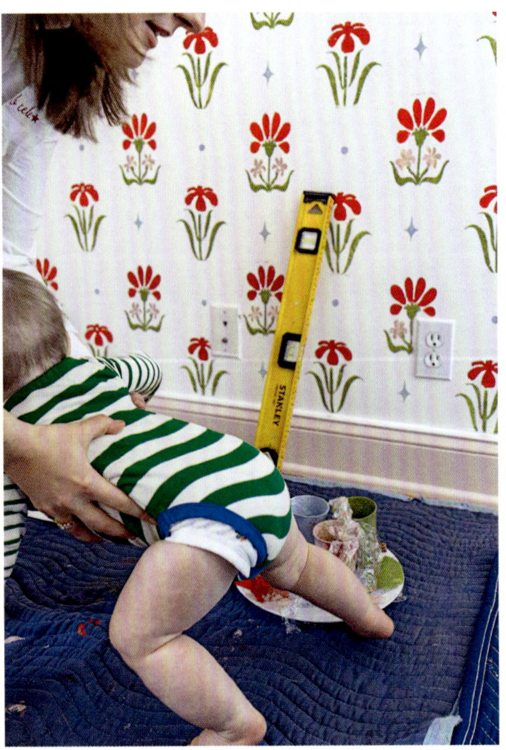

With DIY, chaos reigns.

rather come up with a solution myself than call a handyman in desperation.

You'll have to throw judgment aside for this section and choose humor over second-hand embarrassment. As I said, I'm not perfect. Accidents are a weekly occurrence in my home. When I was sanding in my entryway, I forgot to open any windows. As a result of my transgression, my kitchen looked like the Dust Bowl of 1935. You can't even imagine the guilt and panic that struck me when I realized my baby could be breathing in toxic dust particles. I had to call the pediatrician amid a postpartum shame breakdown to make sure he'd be okay. I hate to break it to you, but just like me, you aren't perfect, either. Therefore, I hope you refer to these next pages over the years when disaster strikes and you'd rather get my advice than call a pro with your tail between your legs.

A
B
USG
SHEETROCK
ALL
URPOSE
C
D
E
F

PATCHING A HOLE

There's an adage that I'd like to emphasize throughout this book: Do as I say, not as I do! I've learned plenty of lessons in my time as an impulsive DIYer, and one of these is *patience*. I've learned to take my time with projects, as it's easier to do things right the first time than to clean up your mistakes after the fact. But sometimes I mess up—and that's okay! I want to impart what I've learned so that you're not facing the same cleanup I've had to deal with myself.

One recent mistake I've made on the job was forgoing any sort of protection on my walls while using a pry bar to take down paneling. While pushing the pry bar into the wall to remove the chair rail, I applied too much pressure, and the pry bar poked a hole right through the drywall!

I immediately thought, *I'm f***ed*. But after a quick Google search, I felt much better about the hole. Turns out, there's a solution!

The hole left behind by my pry bar.

The How-To

MATERIALS

Large putty knife

All-purpose joint compound

Drywall sander

1. With a large putty knife, spread joint compound evenly over your hole (**A**, **B**, **C**, **D**, **E**). Make sure that the wet compound sits above wall level; you'll sand it down after.
2. Wait for the compound to dry.
3. Sand over the patch until it lies even with the wall (**F**). Now you're free to paint over it!

REMOVING TRIM

Sometimes we need to fix what's wrong with our home before we can beautify it. If you have old paneling you don't like, here's an easy recipe for removing it. I'm a huge fan of historic molding, and I'd encourage you to keep it where possible—but this chair rail felt like it was from the nineties and it was in the way of the new paneling I wanted to install. It's much easier to remove than I had assumed, so take a look at how I obliterated this chair rail!

The How-To

MATERIALS

Utility knife

Putty knife

Pry bar

Sandpaper

1. Score the edges of your undesired trim with an X-Acto or utility knife to loosen up the caulk (**A**).
2. Use a putty knife if needed to dig down deeper, creating a larger gap between the wall and trim (**B**).
3. Insert the pry bar into the gap you've created and push the top in to remove the trim (**C**, **D**). Use a putty knife or piece of flat plastic against the wall as you push in the pry bar—don't be like me, who didn't use this precaution and ended up with a hole in my wall!
4. Carefully pull off the trim, being careful of the nails sticking out from the back side (**E**).
5. Sand over the caulk to make the wall totally flat and prepped for painting (**F**).

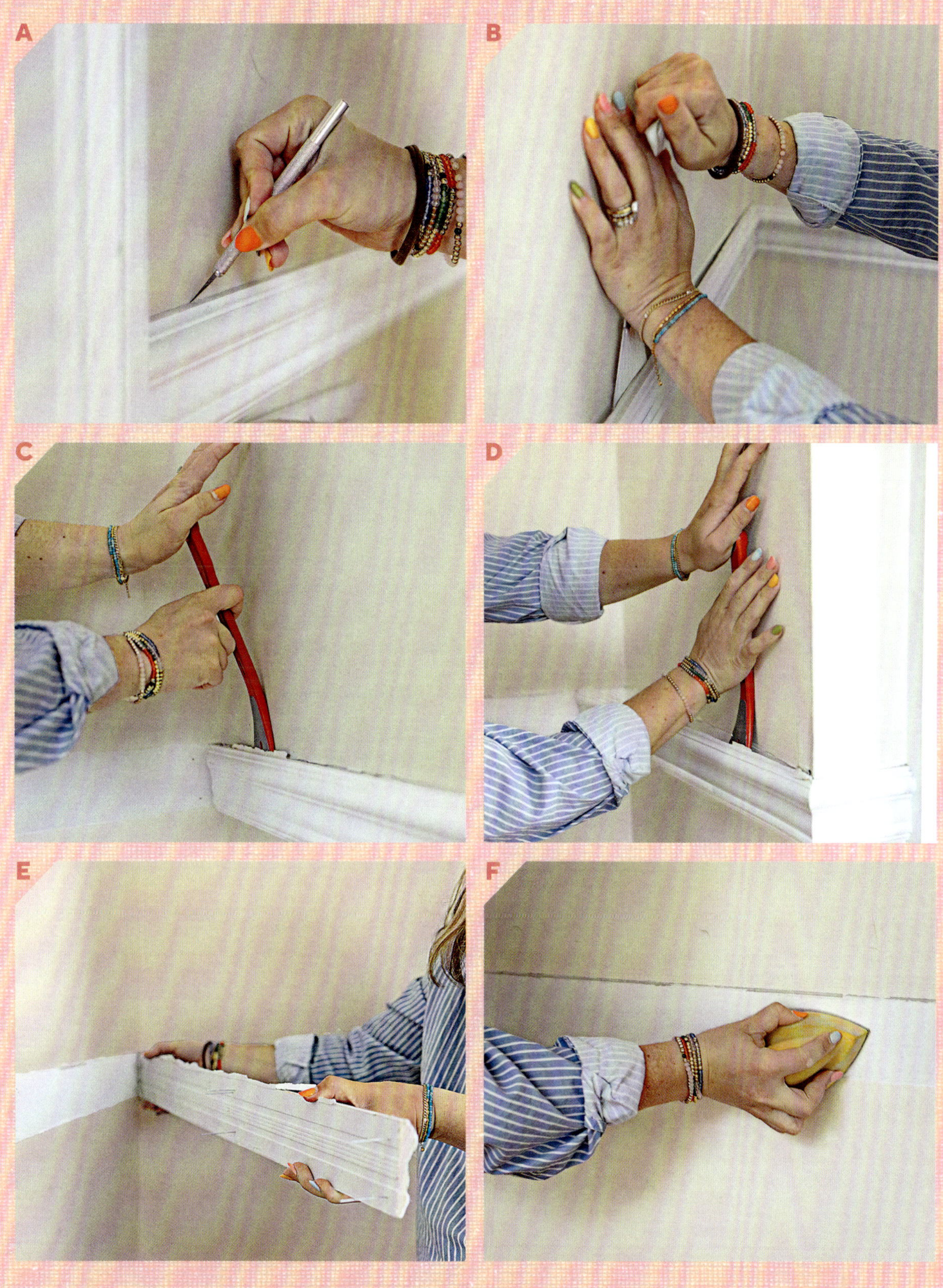
A
B
C
D
E
F

HANG ART WITHOUT F*CKING UP YOUR WALLPAPER

Here's a dilemma: You just spent hours hanging beautiful wallpaper in your room. It looks great, but it's missing something . . . art, of course! I used to hang art over wallpaper without a thought in my head about making a hole in it. But over the years, as my tastes evolved, I'd want to swap one painting for another. But I couldn't just use the old nail—all paintings are created differently, and I'd have to remove the old nail and hammer in a new one, creating so many pinpoint holes that my wallpaper began to resemble the Milky Way.

I wish I'd always stuck to the method I'm going to teach you. It ensures that you'll avoid unsightly holes in your wallpaper when hanging decor.

The How-To

MATERIALS

X-Acto knife

Nails/hooks

1. Measure and mark in pencil the point on the wall where your nail will go.
2. Cut a very small V in your wallpaper with an X-Acto knife around that point.
3. Fold back the V to expose the wall underneath.
4. Hammer in your nail or hook, with the V flipped up.
5. If you ever decide to remove the nail, you'll be able to flip your V down, smoothing it down with a dot of glue. To the naked eye, nobody will know it's been touched!

DEALING WITH A STRIPPED SCREW

I don't know if I hate anything more than the foreboding, hollowed-out center of a stripped screw. If you haven't encountered a stripped screw, congratulations. You're probably a lot less angry of a person than I am. But once you start taking on DIY projects, these little suckers are inevitable. Sometimes you'll find a screw has been stripped by someone else. Maybe you bought a used dresser and need to fix a drawer, only to find that the previous owner was proficient in screw stripping. The more common predicament I find myself in is that I've stripped the screw myself. Either I was trigger-happy with a drill, and let it spin out of control, or used a too-small-size bit. Either way, the issue with a stripped screw is that it is almost impossible to get out. But I'm not writing this book to swap complaints. I recently learned a trick that worked on my first try.

Grab a rubber band and place one side of it over the tip of your screwdriver. Insert the rubber-dressed screwdriver into the naked screw. Did I really just write that? Anyway, you may need to finagle with the size and position of the rubber band to ensure a tight fit into the stripped center. Once it feels tight, slowly twist. If you're not completely *screwed,* this will help loosen it up from the wall!

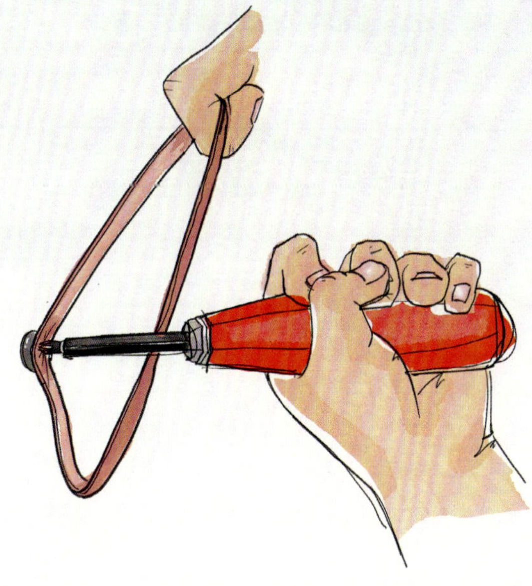

CLEANING UP AFTER A "LANDLORD SPECIAL"

I lived in five different apartments during my New York City era, so I'm very familiar with the dreaded "landlord special." If you rent yourself, you most likely are living among a few landlord oversights and quick fixes yourself. Essentially, landlords must "freshen up" apartments in the short time between tenants. Unfortunately, due to their tendency to be utterly evil (not all landlords are evil, this has just been *my* experience!), landlords clean up their units in the cheapest and fastest way possible. The result is that every surface gets covered in a gunky, hundreds-of-layers-deep coat of paint that lies somewhere yucky on the yellow-to-white spectrum.

No thought is given to prewar architectural details. Doorknobs? Who needs to turn 'em. Paint it all! Trim? Cover up those historic curves with some extra gunk. Oh, that dead fly on the wall? Let's make sure it's *extra* dead and cover it in paint. Its cemented exoskeleton will serve as a beautiful homage to all the humans living among pests in this city. And no, I won't answer your calls or help you deal with those pests. I'm busy painting the entire world my favorite color! LIGHT-PEE YELLOW! I wish I could paint every tree, baby, and animal! Nobody can stop my landlord ways!

The How-To

MATERIALS

- Drop cloth
- Goggles
- Gloves
- Mask
- Drywall sanding blocks
- Wire brush
- Fine-grit sandpaper
- Caulk
- Citrus-based paint stripper
- Paintbrush
- Scraper
- Painter's tape

1. After donning your safety gear and prepping the area with a drop cloth and taping off any walls or floors you don't want stripped, apply your paint stripper with a paintbrush wherever you see fit.

2. Wait until the paint starts bubbling up and cracking. Be patient, and make sure it's finished doing the job. The more work the stripper can do, the less you'll have to scrape!

3. Take out your rage with the scraper. Some sections will be easier than others, coming off like an orange peel. This is so satisfying. When you encounter difficult sections, apply more paint stripper before taking another stab.

4. Address the hardware. If you're looking to clean hardware or hinges, soak them in the stripper until the paint begins peeling off. Then with a wire brush, scrub.

5. Once you've stripped the paint, you may make some archaeological discoveries. Maybe you find wall cracks, holes, or roughness. Take your drywall sanding block and smooth over any rough patches. Caulk any holes or cracks, and sand over it once dried with fine-grit sandpaper.

6. Clean up any powder or caulk residue by wiping the entire area with a damp cloth.

7. Take a break—you deserve some rest after that. Next, you'll repaint the wall the *right* way by following my painting instructions from page 62.

FAR LEFT: When I find a brand I love, there's no changing my mind.

LEFT: Scraping up old paint in my husband's office.

CHAPTER 5

JEWELRY OF THE HOME

I like to imagine decor as the "jewelry of the home" because, just as a watch or necklace serves as the final sparkle you add to complete an outfit, decor is the final step in elevating the stylistic appeal of your living space. You know your aunt who wears bracelets stacked all the way up her arm? You can hear the jingle-jangle of metal clacking together before she even walks through the door. It's her *je ne sais quoi* and goes hand in hand with her exuberant personality. She wouldn't be *her* without her bracelets! Much like accessories transform and complete a chic fashion ensemble, thoughtful decor choices add elegance, charm, and individuality to interiors. Through carefully curated furniture, lighting, textiles, and decorative pieces, your home will become a reflection of your very own tastes, moods, aspirations, and *self*.

SELECTING ART

Keep in mind as you decorate that each choice you make communicates something unique about yourself. If I don't feel a soul tie to a piece of art I see in a store, I'm not buying it! So don't go buying your art at the mall. I struggle to believe that you've actually felt "called" to mass-produced art.

There's a specific piece of mass-produced art that haunts me. I really can't wrap my head around the reasoning behind its commercial success. You may have seen it before. EVERYONE seems to have in their apartment. You MUST know the one: It says so much, while saying so little. I have so many questions about it. I think it's a Highland cow? Maybe it's an ox? Who is the photographer? I hope they've retired to a tropical isle after having made a fortune selling literally millions of the same cow picture. Did they know it'd be such a hit? And why on earth does everyone seem to want that ox picture? I guess I can answer some of those questions myself. It's black and white, though I've also seen it in sepia, which makes it an easy choice for people who claim they "have no style." It fills up a wall without clashing with neutral surroundings. It's kinda funny. His hair is in his eyes. And it's curly. Ha ha. I do get the tendency to go with something you know when it comes to decorating. And if you're buying this ox, you've probably seen it before in a friend's apartment, so it doesn't feel too risky.

Okay, I'm still confused. Why do young Brooklynites and L.A. kids identify so strongly with this animal? So strongly that they'd hang it in their living room? So strongly that it hangs in their living room at a mammoth size, overtaking anything in its path and ruling the room? I just can't shake it. I think we're experiencing an epidemic of mass-produced art taking over our homes. It makes me sad, because there are millions of living artists in the world who sell their work at a fair price. If you head out to galleries or craft fairs, you are bound to find an artist you love. And I bet they sell prints, too—a more affordable option than buying the original.

OPPOSITE: A bright landscape painting adds sparkle and interest to a usually mundane space—the laundry room.

I'm a geek for American Impressionism. I can't stop lurking in online auctions, my finger ready to hit "bid" if ever a piece seems reasonably priced. But I also buy prints, lithographs, and my personal favorite—posters. The posters I like aren't just re-creations of paintings, but instead are actual vintage posters that were used to promote a museum exhibit. I have one for Matisse and two for David Hockney. I feel like I may be coming off like a hoity-toity auction-bidding, gallery-visiting snob, and maybe I am. But I think it's a travesty to hang up a poster that you know is a "safe bet" only because your friend—or that influencer you follow—has the same one.

So promise me you'll look at some art next time you're visiting a new city. Hell, take one of those "what's my favorite art style" quizzes online. Just do some research until you find an artist whose work calls out your name. I'm confident that you can do better than the ox. He's so cute. But you're not an ox farmer.

You know how I said decor is like jewelry? Think of art as earrings. Art is hung above most of your other decor, just as earrings dangle above necklaces and bracelets, and usually art has a silver or gold frame. To dive deeper into this elementary comparison I've made, earrings are the accessory located in closest proximity to your facial features. Earrings should complement and highlight your eyes and draw people in to really *see* you. Art is also the closest anyone can get to truly understanding you through your decor. Art is sensitive, revealing, and evocative. It's highly subjective; there's no good or bad art—because no matter how offputting the color palette or how childlike the lines appear, someone in the world will like it. David Hockney set a record for the highest price paid at auction for a living artist's work when *Portrait of an Artist (Pool with Two Figures)* sold for $90.3 million. I'd pay that! Kidding—but I love his work and can't imagine a world without it. But it's a sure thing that someone out there *hates* David Hockney.

What I'm telling you is that you need to hang the art *you* like. So maybe your brother-in-law scoffed at your Picasso poster, as if he was somehow more cultured than you, or perhaps your dad called your nude oil painting "inappropriate." Guess what? It's not their house. It really doesn't matter what anyone thinks! It took me a long time to accept this. I've spent years putting my videos out to the public, and though I tried to shrug off insults, I couldn't help but take it to heart when an unknown user commented "ur green wall looks like my dog threw up pee soup."

But as I continued to create things *I* found beautiful, I grew a thicker and thicker shell made up of the joy I gained from discovering who I really was. I can proudly say that it's since clicked that *nobody's* opinion about my decor matters aside from my own. Oh, and my husband's, I guess. . . . But thankfully, he's laid-back enough to go with my crazy flow of constant rearranging, impulsive painting, and bizarro ideas. In fact, he seems to enjoy our ever-evolving home style.

So you're not buying the cow poster. Nice! Oh, you thrifted some framed studies of frogs from the 1400s?! Cool! I love frogs, too. And I love that you're embracing all the weird things you love—there's NOTHING cooler than being yourself.

But now that you have some big-kid art, you're not sure exactly where it should go. Let me help.

OPPOSITE: A large nautical painting that can hold its own on my husband's office wall.

A TRUSTY GUIDE FOR HANGING ART

To hang art like a pro, grab a tape measure, level, pencil, and a picture-hanging kit. If your art is crazy big, opt for a screw and anchor to help the hook withstand extra weight. For more guidance on nailing in your art in a precise location, turn to my gallery wall project on page 84.

Pretend you're looking in the mirror. Where do you focus your eyes first? Right at your gorgeous face, correct? When in doubt, eye level is best! I've noticed while silently judging other people's homes that many homeowners hang their art WAY too high. It's an easy mistake to make, and one I often used to make myself. For me, eye level is about 5 feet from the floor. I'm not tall, and I'm not short, so if you aim for that measurement, your art will be at the right level for the average American woman.

This is a rule of thumb that works well in any art-hanging scenario, whether you're hanging a single piece on the wall,

A landscape painting, hung at eye level, grounds a vertical-reaching kitchen.

starting out a gallery wall with your focal piece, or even hanging your art above a piece of furniture.

There are some exceptions, however. If you have very high ceilings, hang your art slightly above eye level so it doesn't look awkwardly low. Another exception has to do with hanging art as part of a vignette over furniture: Say you'd like to hang art above your VERY tall headboard. Due to the headboard's height, you're forced to hang your art above eye level. In this case, you need a different approach. Look for guidelines in the room, like walls and ceilings. In this case, I'd hang the piece halfway between the top of the headboard and the ceiling, so that it feels intentional.

Above desks and dressers, if I'm hanging one big painting, I make sure it isn't wider than my furniture. If it is too wide, I'll give the painting its very own wall.

Eye level is your go-to when hanging artwork.

Speaking of groups, treat a group of paintings as its own larger piece. Place your middle painting at eye level, even if the surrounding pieces will then hang above or below it.

Symmetry is God in the design world. When in doubt, mirror-image it out! I recently hung some art around the TV in my bedroom. I was so satisfied with the result—I hung two bird-study paintings on either side of the TV. Each frame was the same size, and I even made sure that the birds on the left were facing right, and the birds on the right were facing left. All birds led to the TV, and to my bad habit of watching Bravo until two in the morning. We love to see it!

TEXTILES

While art and decor may be the jewelry of the home, textiles are the warm scarf wrapped around your neck, keeping you cozy yet chic on a winter's day. I consider textiles, like flowing curtains, draped quilts, and scalloped shams, on the feminine side of the interior design gender spectrum. More masculine items, in contrast, are angular and abrupt, like wooden tables or metal chairs. I could go on and on about this theory, and even researched it in grad school. My thesis actually included an argument that modernism was a covert attack on femininity. Why else did architects like Mies van der Rohe and Le Corbusier seek to strip all suggestions of ornament, softness, or textile from their modernist designs?

My thesis was called "For Edith," its namesake being Edith Farnsworth, the owner of the infamous Farnsworth House, designed by van der Rohe himself. The house he designed for her was stark and bare, lacking any softness or femininity. Plus, there was no privacy since all exterior walls were glass, AND it flooded. The house went "viral" in the press as Edith and Mies went head-to-head, arguing in angry letters and blowout quarrels. For my thesis, I took Edith on as my own imagined client, and righted the wrongs of her sexist architect, designing her a home that felt draped in softness and privacy by using textile to serve as a nest of security. I felt connected to Edith by the end and hold firmly to the belief that all things associated with femininity are beautiful and should be embraced—not erased!

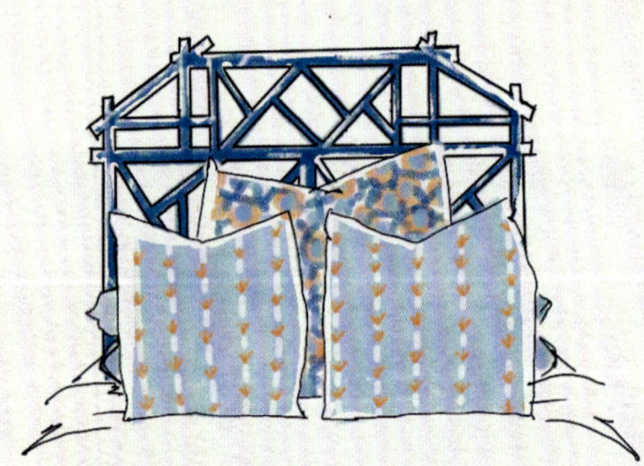

King-, queen-, and twin-size beds with pillows arranged according to the rule of threes.

To tastefully add style to your home through textiles, work with a color palette in mind. Choose one main color for your room, whether it's a new tone you like, or one you can identify already as the strongest in the room. Add two to four complementary tones. These

LEFT: Layering patterns is easy when you stick to different scales. Here, I mixed the small scale floral of the curtain with a larger scale for the wall.

RIGHT: In my son's nursery, a bold yet simple blue-and-white Roman shade feels calm against the busier wallpaper.

can be variants of your dominant color, or different tones that look exciting and cohesive when put together. Use your primary color in larger woven items, like your rug, or the duvet. Source complementary items that are smaller in size. These can be solids or a mixture of your palette. Your room should feel complicated and thoughtful with a diversity of color instead of primary and singular, which can feel juvenile if done incorrectly. I've seen some amazing monochrome rooms, but I'm not even there yet, so unless you're a seasoned designer, I'd focus on a nice mix of color for now!

One question I receive often is "How do I mix patterns without making my decor look too complicated?" Mastering the mix can feel daunting, but if you stick with two to three complementary patterns, you'll be safer than throwing in dozens of prints. Pay attention to scale. Say you're styling throw pillows on your couch. Stick to the rule of threes: one small-scale print, one medium-scale, and one large-scale or solid. Break up the pillows so that your small and large prints are separated by a solid. This breakup of pattern gives your complicated designs some breathing room and gives *you* a place to rest your eye if it ever feels overwhelmed. Plus, having a solid between two patterns ensures that the patterns stand out. To make your vignette extra polished, tie in the solid color with both patterns.

Here's a pattern-mixing example using the rule of threes: Picture a living room with a striped green and cream rug. The stripes are chunky and thick. That's your large-scale pattern. The curtains are a small-scale floral block print, with a palette of pink, neutral, and green. That's your small-scale pattern. See how it ties in with the rug through color, yet differs in scale? Now picture an upholstered ottoman. It's a bold, medium-scaled geometric green pattern, and atop it sits pink, orange, and lilac decor. You notice these secondary colors dispersed throughout the room. The couches are solid neutral, which creates breathing room instead of piling on more pattern. It's all about the mix, but you've got to be careful not to spill when you add in your ingredients!

BABAR
EN
AVION
BABY'S JOURNAL

AESTHETIC FUNCTIONALITY

Some rooms are less decorative by nature. For example, you'll have more knick-knacks and upholstery in your living room than in your kitchen. But you don't need to sacrifice style just because a room serves a more utilitarian function. I like to embrace "aesthetic functionality" when designing areas like this. It's a term I use to describe the method of beautifying even your most utilitarian spaces. The best way to achieve a beautiful look in a functional space is to get creative with your organization. When you think of organizing, you probably think of clear plastic bins, wire baskets, or sticker labels that say PAPER CLIPS. But it doesn't have to be like that! I love finding unique ways to organize items. I bet that if you put your paper clips in a colorful bowl, you'll remember they're in there without a label. Just the association of the colorful container will remind you. It works for even me, who is crippled by ADHD! Of course, wicker baskets are a go-to, but you can get even more creative. What about storing loose coins in a vintage oyster tin? Or reusing glass jars to organize your bathroom, apothecary style! Don't assume you need to spend hundreds or thousands of dollars at The Container Store to have an organized system in your home. Often unexpected containers and items you already own will do the job in a much prettier and more personal way.

OPPOSITE: In my son's room, I decided to forgo unappealing plastic storage drawers, instead opting for a vintage dresser repainted in high-gloss green. Instead of a vinyl changing mat, I used a beautiful basket with waterproof (and washable!) covers.

Bedroom Storage

Books can add color in the unlikeliest of spots. Don't confine them to a bookshelf when they can act as their own decor! Here, a stack of Myles's board books towers whimsically above a wicker elephant.

An antique basket stores my son's towels and extra blankets. Dainty shelves serve as display space for his favorite books.

Laundry Room Storage

Organization can be whimsical! Storing laundry essentials in antique jars and ceramic urns is a functional fix that doesn't sacrifice charm.

For unique storage solutions, shop secondhand! This $10 wire shelf, covered in a beautiful shade of aged green paint, allows my wallpaper to peek through while also offering plenty of smart organization.

To organize these open shelves, I placed a picnic basket atop the highest shelf for storing items I don't need every day, like fancy table linens. Underneath the shelves, I mounted an antique nickel towel bar, which is both prettier and stronger than its modern day plastic counterparts. This provides a neat solution for hanging clothes to dry.

Dear Clare

Every morning when I wake up, I look at my Instagram direct messages. There hasn't been a day in years when I don't receive a question about design. I try to answer as many questions as I can, but it's much more difficult now that I'm balancing my job with motherhood. So in lieu of spending hours glued to my phone answering questions, I thought it'd be helpful to put together a compendium of questions here. All of these questions are Instagram messages I've received from followers. Some are reworded, expanded upon, or even multiple questions put into one to ensure my answer can check as many boxes—and help as many of you—as possible. I focused the advice on the questions I receive *most often*, and only included questions that I haven't already addressed in this book. I hope that you'll find advice to any unanswered queries in this section, and if you don't, please write to me! Your question could be grounds for a second book, or at least inspiration for a new video series!

Dear Clare,

My grandmother recently passed, and I inherited her walnut dresser. I've always loved it in her house, but now that it's in mine, I'm regretting my decision to claim it as my own. It just doesn't fit in! It's a couple hundred years old, and all of my own furniture is jarringly modern in contrast. Do you have any advice for how I can fit this antique piece into my more modern apartment?

Dear Reader,

I recently walked into my living room and realized I'd gone way too far with the antiques. I suddenly experienced an overwhelming sense that I'd time-traveled back to colonial Connecticut: From vintage sailboat paintings, to old wooden boxes, and way too many trinkets from the flea market, there wasn't anything modern in sight! Instead of embracing my inner colonial woman and donning a bonnet to cook biscuits over my fire, I paused to reassess my design choices. I needed some balance. So I walked over to the kitchen, where I've kept more of a modern aesthetic, and grabbed a Matisse poster and some modern pottery. I swapped some of my living room antiques with these modern-day items and it instantly felt much less Early American. That is to say, reader, that I believe you, too, are capable of attaining the right mix of old and new.

With the right strategy, you'll be able to style your grandmother's piece as a stunning focal point that will keep her memory alive—without sacrificing your stylish, modern decor. To bridge the gap between your antique dresser and the rest of the room, dress it up with modern accents. Hang a piece of abstract art or an asymmetrical mirror above it. If the dresser feels too ornate for its surroundings, add minimalist pieces atop it: A simple vase, a modern sculpture, or a stylish bowl will help. To further tie together the room, study the tones of the dresser. I'm imagining it's a deep, warm brown? As you add decor to your space, look for textiles that feature a similar color as an accent. If you're looking to redo your window treatments, perhaps a deep brown velvet would be sexy?

It's also possible that you'll grow to love the historic style of the dresser. Maybe you'll even find antique side tables that pair beautifully with it. You can continue loving modern style while also embracing different eras. Don't play by any rule book, as the best interiors mix all decades together!

Dear Clare,

I want to put wainscoting in my foyer, but it's a rental, so I don't want to lose my security deposit if I cause any damage to the walls. Do you have any tips on how to do it temporarily and not get in trouble?

Dear Reader,

I want to commend you for your bravery. Not many people would be as daring as you—to boldly face a greedy, angry landlord, all in the name of beautiful paneling. You're super cool. I like you. Because I like you, I'm telling you right now: DON'T DO IT! Wainscoting may be worth losing your security deposit over . . . maybe . . . but it's definitely not worth going to court over. If your head can't be turned, and you're set on breaking ground on this project, I always say that it can't hurt to ask. See what your landlord says. He may embrace the idea, and then you're home free! Make sure he puts this in writing.

But there's a chance he'll say no, and then he'll be wary of you and your DIY proclivities until the day you move out. So, I'll say it again, DON'T DO IT—but this time, I present to you an alternative. While at Walmart last week, I found the coolest thing. It was peel-and-stick wallpaper that looked like wainscoting! And it didn't just *look* like wainscoting, it was 3D, so the panels looked super realistic. And, drum roll, I'm not done yet! It was also paintable! And affordable. I bought every roll in stock (with no near-future plans to use it) because I thought it was the bee's knees. So, could we compromise here?

Dear Clare,

We use the hallway bathroom for our newborn baby, but it doubles as a guest bath. Any advice on how to organize the baby's things and make it a fun design for children, but sophisticated enough for adult guests to use?

Dear Reader,

Congratulations on your new arrival. Designing with a baby in the mix always presents new challenges, and yours is a challenge I share! Our guest bathroom doubles as the one closest to the nursery. To make the room feel elevated for your guests, yet special for your child, you're walking a thin design line. Think about this: If you had one room for guests, and one room for your child, what would they look like? How would they be different? In an ideal world, each room in our house could serve a singular use. But this is rarely the case. Right now, my bedroom is half ours, half my baby's. The guest room is half guest room, half closet. The living room doubles as a playroom and changing station. Even my dining room has to accommodate baby stuff, like the stroller that won't fit anywhere else. But we make do. Here's how you can make your baby and your guests comfortable in their shared bathroom. Design a space that feels whimsical and childlike, solely through the colors you choose. Skip any thematic "kiddie" motifs, like rubber-ducky wallpaper or bubble sticker decals on the mirror. If you use bright, playful colors, it will feel fun for your child, and also fun for guests—without overtly looking like a child's bathroom.

Dear Clare,

How can I create a dual-use room? I have a need for both an office and a guest room in my house, but only one space to accommodate both purposes. How can I create a space that feels relaxing for guests despite my office necessities? And how can I create an office that's spacious enough to work in when I also need to have room for a guest bed?

Dear Reader,

You may have read the description of my house from my previous answer, which details how almost every room in my house must serve a dual purpose. I'm in the same boat with my guest room, but instead of an office, it doubles as my closet. The secret to a dual-use room is dual-use design. Think of how every piece of furniture can serve two purposes. You'll need a desk, but if you keep the top clear of coffee cups and file folders, your guest can use it as a vanity. Just place a little mirror on top, which will signal to them that they can feel comfortable enough to sit and get ready there. Instead of the traditional bedside tables flanking the bed, push the bed against a wall to make more room for your workspace. Instead of a bedside table, put a file cabinet for storing your papers. It should be sturdy enough that you can place a lamp on top. When guests come, drape a pretty tablecloth over it to disguise its industrious nature. For storage, divide a dresser in two. Dedicate the bottom drawers to your office supplies, one drawer to guest bed linens, and leave the rest open for guests to use. Write them a nice note to encourage them to use the top three drawers, which will clear up any confusion. You want them to take full advantage of the space without worrying that they're messing up your office. Explaining what's open for them will take care of any worries they may have.

Dear Clare,

My boyfriend and I have opposite tastes. He's not like your husband, who likes how you decorate. I don't want to give up my personal style, but every time I try to hang something up, he hates it! Am I destined to live in an undecorated home for the rest of my life? Should I break up with him over this? I swear, I really love him!

Dear Reader,

Don't fly the unstylish coop just yet. It sounds like you two need to go shopping together. Dedicate an afternoon to go furniture or thrift shopping. Fill up a cart with everything you like. Don't even think about price tags, just fill it! Have him walk around separately and do the same. At the end of your "shopping sprees," compare your carts. Though I doubt that you will both choose the same items, I have faith that as you show him the products in your cart, he may like something! Better yet, you may like the products he picked. Or not. We really don't need to be hanging Bud Light signs in our living room. Sigh. If you're truly decor-incompatible, this assignment will reveal that. Your next attempt would be to mesh your styles. Maybe he's really into golf decor. Ew, but hear me out. Say you love pastel colors and abstract art. The internet is a really, really big place. I bet if you google hard enough, you could find a piece of golf-themed art rendered in the colors you love! If nothing seems to be working, have a real sit-down with him. In my opinion, the individual who has the bigger urge to decorate should be the one leading the decision-making process. It sounds like that person is you. If you're constantly thinking about and stressing over the decor, but he's able to kick his feet up and relax in a stark white apartment, shouldn't you get the first stab at decorating? Also, women are always right. I should have just written that instead of this whole paragraph.

Dear Clare,

I hate my kitchen but can't do anything about it. I rent an apartment with nineties-style warm oak kitchen cabinets. I hate the color, but I'm too afraid of the ramifications of painting. Is there anything I can do to make this kitchen cuter?

Dear Reader,

You're going to think I'm crazy, but hear me out: Embrace the oak cabinets. I know they're ugly. I know they hurt your eyes. They're sad. I get it. I do. But if you can't paint them, join them! Isn't that what they say? You're going to have to learn to love them. Or even like them. Okay, maybe just feeling neutral about them will be better than what you feel right now. Here are some things you can do to modernize those cabinets. First, get a peel-and-stick backsplash tile in a cool tone to balance the warmth of the oak color. Try a faux Carrara marble. I actually like this stuff—I put fake subway tile up in my first Upper West Side apartment, and it lasted for the duration of our lease. It also didn't leave any residue. Don't buy the peel-and-stick tile that's made of actual STONE. I learned from experience that cleaning it up is nearly impossible, and it leaves behind a permanent coat of gloop. In terms of the cabinets themselves, ask your landlord if you can sand and stain them a darker or lighter color. I doubt he (or she) will oblige, but you never know. Either way, purchase new hardware. I can picture yours now. My crystal ball is showing me a dull nickel finish. It's clunky, neither modern nor classic. It's got to go. Buy new hardware you love that feels modern in contrast to the cabinets. And learn from my mistakes! Store your old hardware in a safe and marked location so you know where it is when it comes time to move.

Dear Clare,

There's a small hallway in my home that is SO boring. I want every corner of my house to be cute, but the awkwardly tiny size of the hallway makes it hard to decorate. What should I do?

Dear Reader,

This calls for stripes! Stripes make me feel like a total magician. Want to widen a room? Horizontal stripes! Want to make your ceilings look taller? Vertical stripes! Painting them is cheaper than wallpapering them, and you're in luck because you're working in a small area. That means less work. If you really want to have fun with the space, continue the stripes onto the ceiling so the area feels like a special little jewel box of beauty! Use a ruler at the top and bottom of your wall to mark off evenly where your stripes will land. Run a straight line of painter's tape from the top mark to the bottom to create one side of your stripe. Measure the thickness you want and run a line down for the other side. Use a template to create a consistent thickness throughout so that each stripe is polished and identical to the one next to it.

Dear Clare,

I hate my bathroom. It has no natural light and feels like a total cave. The only window is just a "legality" and was built there so the landlord doesn't get in trouble. It literally looks directly at the brick wall of the building next to mine. The tile is a dark gray with disgusting grout. How can I make the bathroom a space I like? I dread going in there to shower!

Dear Reader,

Let me tell you a story about my first apartment in New York City. I went in with two college friends, thinking we'd find a decent three-bedroom within the boundaries of Manhattan for just $1,000 each. What can I say? I lived in Worcester, Massachusetts, before moving to New York—I was totally clueless! Turns out, we could find an apartment. But it was a ONE-bedroom. The only way to make it work was for one roommate to pay about $500 more and get the big room. The other two could live at a discounted rate—and a discounted quality of life—in the living room we split in half. One bedroom got a few inches more than the other due to the placement of the living room window, and one didn't have a window at all. Guess which room I opted for? I'll give you a hint: My salary was the lowest and my parents didn't help. I still can't believe I made it work for almost six months in that windowless doom room. Finally the cockroaches and bedbugs drove us downtown. I couldn't have been happier to leave that place, my jail cell of a bedroom, and the bathroom I dreaded going into. I really do feel your pain—the bathroom didn't have a window, and if it did and I've blocked it from my memory, it was definitely facing a brick wall like yours does. If I had any DIY wits about me back then (I didn't—it took me and two friends an entire night to put together a console table that quickly broke because we'd assembled it wrong), I would have pulled a couple of tricks to make the bathroom more livable. That is, if I was forced to be there any longer than I had to be. First, I would spend an entire day deep-cleaning it. That way, you can feel better about the cosmetic Band-Aid you'll be putting over the grossness. Then I'd swap out the lighting for bulbs that are more welcoming. I'd buy some subway-style white peel-and-stick tile and coat the entire shower with it. Then I'd do the same to the floor, with bigger hexagonal or square shapes. This will hopefully brighten it up, and you'll have surfaces you aren't so afraid to touch. And, by the way, when is your lease up?

Dear Clare,

I'm in the midst of redoing a 1980s ranch. The walls are a poo-colored brown paneling, and I have no natural light. Tell me what to do!

Dear Reader,

A xylophile, according to a very recent Google search, is someone who loves wood. So, xylophiles, ignore what I'm about to say here. I like wood, but I'm not commenting on others' social media posts in angry capital letters when I see someone paint over wood furniture. For some reason, there's a group of wood-loving fanatics out there who become absolutely enraged if they see anyone get near wood with a paintbrush. Me? I shrug. Humans have been painting wood for as long as paint has existed. It's what we do. And it sounds like we aren't working with gorgeous turn-of-the-century carved oak here. So paint it! Even worse, paint it white! I can feel their violent shuddering from here. But seriously, painting ugly wood paneling is the simplest way to take your walls from dive-bar pool room to clean, shabby-chic freshness. Don't feel guilty. Any wood paneling or furniture built post-1940 is fair game to be painted.

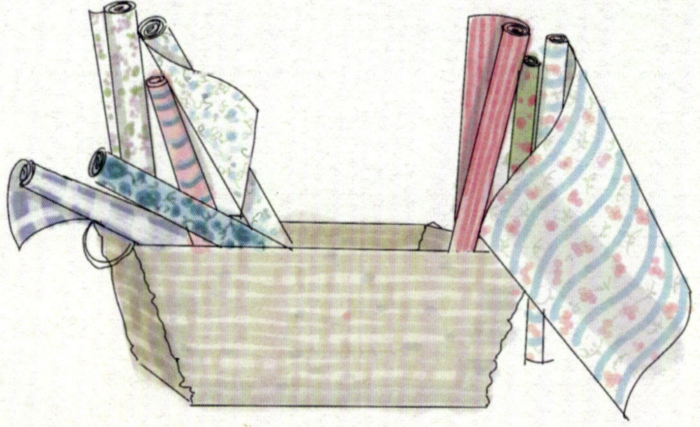

APPENDIX

SHOPPING FOR FURNITURE AND DECOR—CLARE'S FAVORITES

Online

FACEBOOK MARKETPLACE

When I don't want to deal with the high price of shipping a furniture purchase, I always check Facebook Marketplace first. Actually—I check it daily. To find what you're looking for, use search terms that describe what you have in mind. Instead of searching "desk," which will bring up hundreds of different styles and levels of wear, write phrases that describe what you're looking for. Search for "midcentury modern oak secretary desk" or "scrubbed pine French vintage desk." There's *nothing* like scoring what you're looking for right in your hometown! Just be prepared to pick up the item. If you don't have a pickup truck or large vehicle, often sellers will bring your buy to you at a discounted delivery price. Make sure that before you buy the item, you've inspected it to ensure that you're happy with your purchase.

CHAIRISH

This site is definitely Budget *Luxury,* meaning that they sell truly luxurious designer pieces for less than what you'd pay for new. That said, it's fairly expensive! There won't be many cheap finds here, but you can be confident that what you're buying is high-quality. They have a fabulous curated selection of art and decor and offer white-glove delivery.

EBAY

I'm an auction addict, so my laptop usually has tabs open for items I'm "watching" on eBay. One tactic I employ to avoid high shipping costs is to use filters that target local listings. My husband is a big vintage clothing shopper on eBay. He's actually over my shoulder right now, pestering me to look at the shirt he found on eBay that arrived today. "The eBay Bandit's back at it again!" I was confused, given that I'm currently writing an appendix item about eBay. Did he know? Nope, just a weird coincidence. Or maybe not, given that both of us love shopping secondhand and admittedly do it often. I turned around, and he was proudly standing in a long-sleeve gorgeous navy collared shirt. I asked him what brand it was. "Purple Label. Ralph Lauren. New with tags and it was originally $450." He paid $79! This obsession began when he found a Brioni blazer on eBay by chance. If you're wondering what this brand is, just know that we are NOT the kind of people who can wear Brioni. The blazer was originally seven THOUSAND dollars. He paid $300, and wears it way too often, always making sure to "casually" mention who made it. If you're not looking for menswear, eBay is just as good for finding designer or at least "high design" home goods and decor. I like it for art and smaller items, because shipping can get complicated and expensive with furniture. I also use eBay as a tool while I'm out thrifting. If I find something I like that seems pricey, I'll check eBay for "listing" and "sale" prices to compare. eBay also offers authentication services for many of their product categories.

ETSY

My go-to place for buying custom-sized ANYTHING! You can find custom Roman shades, custom bamboo blinds, custom drapes, and even valances. Search the style you're looking for, like "block printed" or "boho" or "abstract" + "custom" + the product you need, like "pleated curtains" or even "rug." You'll be astonished at your options!

In-Person

CONNECTICUT

MONGERS MARKET

This gigantic indoor flea is in Bridgeport, Connecticut. Its only downfall is that Mongers is open only on Sundays. Plan to spend a few hours there. There is parking, a café, and an ATM onsite, and you need to purchase a $3 ticket to get in. The place is huge. It's great for standard antiquing, but it's also the best for architectural salvage, like old doors and windows, columns, vintage hardware, and even interior molding!

FAIRFIELD COUNTY ANTIQUE AND DESIGN

This antiques mall in Norwalk, Connecticut, is a favorite for interior designers to find unique items for their clients. It's great for rattan and bamboo furniture, lacquered items, and interesting yet tasteful decor. Most of the sellers have fabulous taste or are designers themselves, so if you're looking for a curated "flea market" experience, this is the place for you. Note that prices will be demonstrably higher than your average flea.

FLORIDA

DEVONSHIRE OF PALM BEACH

This Palm Beach treasure isn't a thrift store by any means. It's actually an extremely well-curated and relatively expensive antiques store, but I insist that if you're ever in South Florida, you make the trip. Their collection of items includes a worldwide selection of antiques from Morocco, Italy, France, and South Africa. You may be able to pick up a deal on small items, but if not, you'll leave feeling *very* inspired.

SNAPPY TURTLE HOME

Yes, I'm biased—this is the store founded by my Mimi and owned and operated today by my aunts. If you're ever in Delray Beach, tell them I sent you! My aunt does a fabulous job stocking a wide variety of exquisite home decor items at a variety of prices.

CIRCA WHO FURNITURE

If Palm Beach is the epicenter of colorful, tropical, Hollywood Regency meets chinoiserie opulence, Circa Who is its capital! Here you'll find beautiful antiques that have been refinished with fresh lacquer or reupholstered with designer fabric. They have a huge inventory, so you're likely to find what you need here!

WORLD THRIFT

This Lake Worth thrift store is gigantic and has an insane variety of items. Get there early, as competition is steep. Check online to see what special offers they're putting on for the week. Often they'll have big sales on specific days.

MAINE

ANTIQUES USA

This is the indoor equivalent of the Arundel Flea Market, and it sits just across the road! Hundreds of booths sit occupied for your perusal. My dad actually sells out of a few of them—look out for snowshoes, the vintage Gucci loafers he still hasn't sold, and nautical paraphernalia.

THE ARUNDEL FLEA MARKET

If ever you find yourself in my home state of Maine, make sure to stop off Route 1 and spend a weekend morning at my favorite flea market in the whole world. Okay, so I haven't been to the Paris Flea yet, but maybe if I sell enough of these books I'll be able to travel to Paris and make the comparison! There's a wonderful café on the premises—try the avocado toast or bubble tea. You'll need the fuel for walking through the long rows of tables! Get there early—I mean before 7 A.M. early—if you don't want to miss the good finds. You'll have to beat my dad, who I know is cursing me for encouraging more shoppers to compete with him.

MARDEN'S

In my family, we say "Marden's Miracle!" when referring to anything found at Marden's for a great price. The real slogan? "I should have bought it when I saw it at MARDEN'S!" And it's true. You'll have buyer's regret if you don't jump on the bandwagon. Insanely cheap designer fabric, criminally low-priced furniture, and don't skip the shoe section.

NEW YORK

HOUSING WORKS

The best thing about Housing Works, a New York City–based thrift shop chain, is that you can feel proud of the purchases you make—it's a nonprofit organization whose mission is to fight both AIDS and homelessness. Their merchandise comes mainly from donations, so you never know what you may find. Often they'll have designer items. You never know what a crazy old Manhattanite deems "trash"! I've found glassware, plates, great old books, and baskets.

OLDE GOOD THINGS

This store has a great selection of old chairs, desks, lighting, and coffee tables. They also have interesting and unexpected finds, like stone busts, brass hardware, doorknobs . . . you name it!

USA-WIDE

ESTATE SALES

When traveling, if I have some extra room in the trunk of my car, I'll check the town's online newspaper. Take a look in their classifieds section, and you may find a list of the weekend's estate, yard, or garage sales. This is most beneficial when you're in a fancy place. I have had great luck in the Hamptons and Maine.

GOODWILL

You never know what you'll find when you walk in, but I prefer shopping for smaller home items here, like glassware, dishes, and collectible china. I often see Blue Willow china here, which is a personal favorite!

HABITAT FOR HUMANITY

Habitat is another chain store that you can feel positive about—it's a nonprofit also based on donations. With the earnings they make from selling these donations, the organization creates housing and shelter in their local community for those in need. Donations include antiques and small items, but the cool thing about Habitat is that they also accept anything from kitchen cabinets to pedestal sinks—even toilets are acceptable! So if you're looking for a slab of marble or a light fixture—or anything big for your home—you may strike it lucky at Habitat.

STENCILING TEMPLATES

Use these stencil templates as your very own by placing plastic acetate paper over the image and tracing with a permanent marker. Then cut along the lines. *Note:* All objects filled in with color are intended to be *removed* from the design. These areas will be colored in with your paint!

If you're stenciling a tile floor, you may need a different size than those included in this appendix. I recommend scaling the stencil using a copy machine or uploading a photo of it to your computer so you can scale it to any size before tracing it.

ACKNOWLEDGMENTS

With the insular nature of my work, on some afternoons, in the midst of craft projects and the pressure of the setting sun taking away my filming light, I feel that I am on an island. But after the earth rotates far enough counterclockwise that my camera turns grainy, after the babysitter hands me my hungry son, after the shih tzus sing their evening siren song when my husband opens the door, I remember that I'm not an island. I'm lucky enough to be on the mainland, buoyed by my friends and family whose support I feel wholly undeserving of.

To Brian: If I am the sail, you are the anchor of our ship. If I am the swaying weathervane of an old house, you are the foundation. If I am the smiling stewardess, you are the steering pilot. On paper, we make perfect sense, but in the grand scheme of "what-ifs," I consider finding you, and getting to keep you, to be the most miraculous gift that I've been given. Thank you for giving me direction, laughter, and butterflies. Thank you for helping me feel my best each and every day. Chickens.

To my mom: Thank you for raising me to believe in fairies, to observe and appreciate the small, beautiful parts of our visual world, and for demonstrating the importance of kindness, curiosity, and wit. Thank you for making me write, even during the summer when school wasn't even in session. You are the most beautiful woman alive, and the smartest person I know. Thank you for always helping me, and for saying the right thing when I need guidance. And thanks for giving me Aidan, the best brother of all time.

To my dad: You are my inner voice, guiding my choices, goals, and behavior. I'm more like you than anyone on earth, and I wouldn't have it any other way. Thank you for showing me what life looks like when you pursue your own joy. When you pick yourself up by the bootstraps. When you "suck it up." We all know you're proud of me, but I'd like you to know that I'm proud of *you:* the way you made yourself captain of your own life at such a young age, from spraying gunite pools in high school to fishing for king crab in Alaska, you've never shied away from hard work. From your entrepreneurial tenacity to the way you dive headfirst into your passions, I am so proud to call you my dad.

To my Aunty Caroline: Every week, you asked me for an update on my book. I've never heard of an aunt who cares so deeply and honestly for her niece. You, Aunty M, and Mimi gave me the strength (and blueprint) to dress and decorate with a bold selfishness that defines "cool."

To Nikki, the childhood hometown elementary school classmate turned book photographer, who, in the midst of my pregnancy and craziness of becoming a new mom, became my right-hand woman. Thank you for your support. You bring my ideas to beautiful light. Your skills reach beyond the technical and into a deep well of resourcefulness, beauty, aesthetic understanding, and care. You're everything that this book stands for.

To Brittany, Leigh, and Dervla: Thank you for believing in my big idea and, in the process, being patient with me, encouraging me, and supporting me with kindness during this year of head-spinning change.

To my girlfriends: I promise I'll call you back in 2026 once I get my head above water! (JK—but actually, I love each and every one of you. Thank you for your jokes, for your fun, for your love.)

To James "Jamie" Salomon, who we lost too soon, and his family. Thank you, Jamie, for your invigorating enthusiasm, your wealth of knowledge, and the laughs we shared during those days of shooting the book together. It was an honor to me that you'd give my project a chance, given your prolific career. I will always admire you and cherish the images you took—you turned the mundane into graceful and atmospheric beauty.

ILLUSTRATION AND PHOTO CREDITS

All photos not credited here are by Nikki Hirst
All illustrations not credited here are by Clare Sullivan
Photos by Jamie Salomon: pp. 70, 72, 76, 77, 78, 92, 110, 120, 126, 130, 134, 136, 137, 138
Photos by Sergey Sevastyanov: p. 160
Shutterstock/Sirina F (tape): pp. 1, 38, 70, 128, 216, 234, 272
Shutterstock/My Life Graphic (multiple papers): pp. 4, 17, 27, 29, 30, 43, 64, 88, 97, 100, 116, 144, 170, 171, 176, 178, 192, 206
Shutterstock/rangizzz (photo frame): p. 5
Shutterstock/CCVideo (photo frame): p. 5
Shutterstock/Krasovski Dmitri (photo frame): p. 5
Shutterstock/Cadded Designs (flower pattern): pp. 6–7
Shutterstock/Lifestyle Graphic (paper): pp. 6, 7, 70, 51, 54, 57, 61, 83, 86, 94, 95, 112, 126, 142, 150, 168, 190, 223, 229, 235, 236, 244, 251, 258, 259, 260, 261, 269, 270
Shutterstock/Kwangmoozaa (paper): p. 10
Shutterstock/Valery Evlakhov (tape): pp. 11, 43, 45, 54, 56, 61, 62, 69, 70, 72, 76, 79, 86, 88, 91, 96, 99, 100, 103, 106, 114, 117, 118, 122, 128, 132, 136, 139, 143, 144, 148, 150, 152, 178, 187, 197, 203, 204, 205, 206, 209, 210, 216, 225, 226, 231, 232, 234, 237, 247, 250, 251
Shutterstock/Olga Kovalenko (paperclip): p. 16
Shutterstock/Cadded Designs (floral pattern): p. 16
Shutterstock/Ragnarock (paper): pp. 16, 36, 37, 38, 39, 58, 74, 75, 151, 169, 209, 210, 240, 246, 247, 262
Shutterstock/David M. Schrader (paper): pp. 24, 25, 26, 28, 31, 252, 253, 254, 255, 256, 257
Shutterstock/Marish (ornamental border): pp. 24, 25, 26, 28, 31, 252, 253, 254, 255, 256, 257
Shutterstock/Nadia Gallegos (blue polka dot tape): p. 34
Shutterstock/onair (paper): pp. 34, 35, 37, 69, 105, 120, 121, 147, 160, 171, 197, 206, 214, 226, 250, 271, 272
Shutterstock/lalec (patterned background): pp. 36–37
Shutterstock/Tymonko Galyna (yellow tape): p. 37
Shutterstock/P.NOONIN (staples): pp. 37, 56, 62, 70, 76, 86, 88, 92, 96, 100, 106, 110, 116, 120, 125, 126, 130, 132, 134, 135, 140, 142, 144, 147, 150, 176, 192, 197, 203, 204, 205, 216, 237, 247, 250, 251
Shutterstock/anna1195 (patterned background): pp. 38–39
Shutterstock/Intellson (Post-it note): pp. 44, 55, 63, 92, 93, 107, 110, 111, 120, 121, 126, 127, 130, 131, 134, 135, 141, 171
Shutterstock/ESB Professional (paper with tape): pp. 43, 96, 173, 183; (blue paper) 114
Shutterstock/Lifestyle Graphic (graph paper): pp. 45, 62, 64, 72, 76, 79, 88, 91, 96, 99, 100, 103, 106, 109, 114, 117, 118, 122, 125, 128, 132, 136, 139, 140, 143, 144, 148, 152, 187, 231, 232, 234, 237
Shutterstock/pics five (silver thumbtacks): pp. 6, 7, 55, 61, 64, 70, 86, 112, 126, 132, 136, 148, 150, 151, 176, 187, 203, 223, 236, 246, 247, 250, 269, 270
Shutterstock/Mega Pixel (brass thumbtacks): pp. 57, 69, 94, 95, 105, 109, 142, 151, 176, 197, 204, 205, 216, 220, 235, 244, 245, 251, 258, 259, 260, 261
Shutterstock/Darya Kozlovskikh (tropical pattern): p. 58
Shutterstock/karen roach (index card with paperclip): pp. 64, 168
Shutterstock/Textile Artwork (floral pattern): pp. 74, 75
Shutterstock/Wachiwit (tape): pp. 82, 170, 171, 176, 229, 272
Shutterstock/Rawpixel.com (tape): pp. 49, 64, 83, 114, 142, 164, 214, 244, 261
Shutterstock/Sirina F (tape): pp. 128, 169, 234
Shutterstock/Leaf2Tree Studio (flower pattern): p. 160
Shutterstock/Tymonko Galyna (blue tape): pp. 167, 201
Shutterstock/Serge Zimniy (pattern): p. 169, 170, 171
Shutterstock/pics five (paper with tape): p. 174
Shutterstock/PrintUp Studio (striped pattern): pp. 246–47
Shutterstock/pashabo (paper with scalloped edge): pp. 252–57
Shutterstock/Fat Cat Happy Studio (flower pattern): pp. 258–59
Shutterstock/hashtag cads (patterned background): pp. 260–61

CLARE SULLIVAN is an interior designer, artist, and content creator. She lives in Connecticut with her husband, son, and shih tzus.

NIKKI HIRST is a self-taught photographer based in Brooklyn. Her work is focused on shining a light on the beautiful aspects of everyday life and is centered at the intersection of home and memory.